T0113555

Higher Ground

Enjoying A Closer Walk With God

Olayinka Dada, M.D.

authorHOUSE®

AuthorHouse™
1663 Liberty Drive
Bloomington, IN 47403
www.authorhouse.com
Phone: 833-262-8899

© 2020 Olayinka Dada, M.D. All rights reserved.

No part of this book may be reproduced, stored in a retrieval system, or transmitted by any means without the written permission of the author.

Published by AuthorHouse 08/04/2020

ISBN: 978-1-7283-6708-8 (sc)
ISBN: 978-1-7283-6707-1 (e)

Library of Congress Control Number: 2020915010

Print information available on the last page.

Any people depicted in stock imagery provided by Getty Images are models, and such images are being used for illustrative purposes only. Certain stock imagery © Getty Images.

This book is printed on acid-free paper.

Because of the dynamic nature of the Internet, any web addresses or links contained in this book may have changed since publication and may no longer be valid. The views expressed in this work are solely those of the author and do not necessarily reflect the views of the publisher, and the publisher hereby disclaims any responsibility for them.

Scripture quotations marked NKJV are taken from the New King James Version. Copyright © 1982 by Thomas Nelson, Inc. Used by permission. All rights reserved.

Scripture quotations marked NIV are taken from the Holy Bible, New International Version®. NIV®. Copyright © 1973, 1978, 1984 by International Bible Society. Used by permission of Zondervan. All rights reserved. [Biblica]

Scripture quotations marked GNT are taken from the Good News Translation — Second Edition. Copyright © 1992 by American Bible Society. Used by permission. All rights reserved.

Scripture quotations marked MSG are taken from THE MESSAGE. Copyright © 1993, 1994, 1995, 1996, 2000, 2001, 2002, 2003 by Eugene H. Peterson. Used by permission of NavPress Publishing Group. Website.

CONTENTS

DEDICATION

To Timothy Inioluwa, my loving son; it is a delight watching you grow from a newborn to a young man. I pray your life and legacy will be bigger and better than mine.

ACKNOWLEDGEMENTS

To the only wise God, my King and Lord, I am indebted to you for life for your goodness and tender mercies towards me.

Daddy and mommy Adeboye. Your love, time and tutelage are greatly appreciated.

Oluwatoyin Abimbola, my heartthrob, your dedication, resourcefulness and productivity are unparalleled. I love you greatly.

Inioluwa, Oreoluwa, Adeoluwa and Opeoluwa. My lovely children. Thank you for not giving up despite the pressures you experienced as pastor's kids. Your desires to know God and deep worship are ongoing inspirations and excitements for me.

To every member of Restoration House Family, I salute your loyalty and dedication to the gospel of our Lord and Saviour Jesus Christ.

INTRODUCTION

A great man of God once shared a dream where he saw many job seekers lined up in front of a recruiting company; each person with great qualifications. Then the chairman of the recruiting company selected some of the job seekers and instructed them to follow him. As they walked along the halls of the vast industrial complex, some of the job seekers saw their departments of interest and decided to stop following the chairman and joined the workforce of these departments on their own without being employed or assigned.

Eventually, others followed suit and the group following the man dropped in number to the one man who followed him to his office. The chairman then asked him why he did not follow his colleagues. He responded by saying, "Your last command was for us to follow you and I was determined to do just that unless instructed otherwise by you." Pleased with this response, the chairman ushered him into a bigger complex that was designed for new managerial level workers. He also explained to him that the previous complex where the other recruits went was designed for casual workers and as such, new workers would not get paid because they labored in the wrong place. These new recruits ended up being let go except for the man who had followed the chairman's instructions. This book is essentially about paying attention to instructions that are designed to lead us in the right direction or to a higher ground; you will do well to follow through!

God's plan for man is to reign and rule in righteousness for His glory. He endowed man with power to achieve greatness and be properly positioned in exercising dominion over God's creation. God desires fellowship with His children and also for them to experience and enjoy new and better things in their lives. This is one of the reasons the Bible says His mercies are new every morning (Lamentations 3:22-23 NKJV).

God wants to expose us to greater experiences beyond our imaginations. I am convinced that one of the major problems limiting the advancement of many people in life is underexposure. I personally discovered that exploring new relationships, environments, skills, challenges, etc., increases my faith and inspirations beyond comprehension. God does not want us to live a stale and dull life; He rather wants us to live an eternal and promising one.

God is calling His children to a higher ground. Don't be stuck with your present state! There are better, bigger and newer opportunities for exploits, newer revelations, newer ideas, newer information, newer inventions and newer songs that He wants to expose us to.

Then the Lord said to Moses, "Come up to me on the mountain and be there; and I will give you tablets of stone, and the law and commandments which I have written, that you may teach them." (Exodus 24:12 NKJV)

The journey to higher ground is often a response to divine instructions. When we aspire to higher grounds as God's children, we are in effect obeying a call to greatness and maximized living. Hence, a higher ground is a place where we are drawn closer to God. Any height that is void of this reality is godless and, in essence, a bottomless pit. This is simply because God will not invite you to a place that is void of His presence. Receiving an invitation to execute a contract or benefitting from a privilege where the principles and priorities are void of God's hand is almost certainly guaranteed to lead anywhere but a higher ground. People tend to assume that every elevated status in life is tantamount to higher grounds. However, it is clear that the presence of God is what makes any place a higher ground. To climb the ladder of success and yet be distant from God's presence will only end in disappointment. Some people naturally distance themselves from God and His kingdom principles as soon as they become rich or famous. Higher ground cannot simultaneously boost your bank account and deplete you spiritually. From the text above, the following lessons and features of a higher ground can be drawn from a careful observation of God's invitation to Moses:

Be There (Presence)

A higher ground is not a washroom or a place of convenience where one rushes in for a quick relief and dashes out to the status quo. God told Moses to "be there." Hence, a higher ground is a divine location, a place of personal encounter with the only true God. The location for receiving life's crown is often void of the crowd; a place of separation, a place where one's heart and convictions are settled. One can still live a fulfilled life without participating in or enjoying the social activities and ceremonies of this life.

There are people who missed their college's matriculation ceremony, yet still went on to make positive impacts on the society. You also don't need to dine with royalty in order to leave your footprints on the sands of time. There is, however, a place where you need to be; a place where God specifically designates and marks out for your life and, you need to make conscious effort to "be there." Hence, you need to identify the place and be there. Only then can you be bold to claim you have found the higher ground. It's not a place to be by proxy. No, you have to be there in person, with total concentration and devotion. To you, this is the place called THERE! It's your location of personal encounter and intimacy with the Lord.

There are so-called Christians today who cannot boldly approach God in faith for pressing needs in their lives unless they consult a prophet. Such people are yet to arrive on the higher ground. Relating with God through prophetic can be safely considered one of the symptoms of living in a low spiritual ground.

Tablets of Stone (Presents)

In ancient times, tablets were carved and smoothened from stone for the purpose of writing. Imagine what the tablets God gave to Moses would be worth in today's currency if they're to be auctioned off for sale! How much would people offer just to see or touch them just so they can have a feel of

God's handwriting? It is a known fact that ancient paintings tend to attract fortunes at auctions today, how much then would God's ancient "iPad" be worth? Anyone living at the low spiritual ground is exposed to corruptible and transient things, but the one on higher ground has access to original and durable things from God. On the higher ground, you're enriched with divine and invaluable treasures. Your life cannot be empty when you are on the higher ground. Most of the lacks we experience in life are reflections of our realms of operation. The higher ground may not bring you earthly riches, but your life will abound with spiritual blessings in heavenly places and, heavenly places are not empty places! If you're experiencing any form of emptiness, you need to locate and relocate to your higher ground.

The Law and Commandments (Principles)

One of the pieces of evidences for operating on the higher ground is that you live your life based on the principles of God's law and commandments. A godless man is a lawless man. On the higher ground, you're not tossed about by every wind of doctrine or emotional manipulations, rather, you're properly anchored on the principles of God's words. These principles influence your marriage, ministry, businesses, relationships and life's pursuits. Those on the lower can easily be derailed from their purpose and dreams because they're like vehicles without their braking system.

Teach Them (Purpose)

The higher ground is also a place where purpose can be revealed. This is evident in God's invitation to Moses for a personal encounter on Mount Sinai. There, Moses received gifts and revelations of certain life's principles that are designed to fulfill particular purposes and, in this case, "That you may teach them." A man's purpose tends to get clearer as he ascends to his higher ground. Having a clouded mind and being confused about what to do with God's gifts in your life is an indication that you're yet to reach your higher ground. It's also on the higher ground that God's commandments are unveiled to us and where we received the burden to teach others the same.

What does your life reflect to others about ministry, marriage, business, compassion, etc.? A life that is void of righteousness, holiness, excellence, integrity, commitment, loyalty, and sacrifice, is considered a lower ground life. A higher ground life is always worthy of emulation, both in words and deeds. A higher ground life offers solutions to difficult situations, not complicate them.

Coming From the Ground

And the Lord God formed man of the dust of the Of all things created by God to live on the earth, it is only the man formed from the ground that carries the breath of God. Hence, every man created by God has his origin and history with the ground. Now that we're born again, the nature of God is still being formed in us until we fully partake of His divine nature. If we refuse to be formed by God, we deny ourselves access to the breath of God and the essence of living. We may exist, but not living the life we were created to live; a life of impact both in time and space.

Every great man started from the ground up, but did not end there. Two major differences between great men and ordinary men can be traced to their formation and their source of inspiration. Men who became great are men who have allowed God to form them, using the dusty materials and experiences of the ground to open them up to divine inspirations that make them valuable souls to the world. Living marriages, living ministries, living businesses and living careers, are products of souls that have been infused with divine breath. Some troubled marriages and ministries have sucked the life out of others simply because they're composed of dead souls.

We need to become living souls before we can start producing life! It's impossible to give what you don't have themselves to be formed by being exposed, expressly or by implication, to the molding hands of God. This formation granted them access to God's breath of ideas, thereby giving life to their researches and investigations. Function is an offspring of formation. When the Bible says that man became a living soul, it means he became functional as God originally intended. In life, you cannot function effectively until you're first formed. God's inspiration connects your formation with your function. The natural implication of God's breath was that man instinctively became functional.

The fall of man in the garden led to humanity's deformation. Man became flawed in Eden as a result of his disobedience and was consequently sentenced to till the ground. He became estranged from the One who gave him breath and couldn't function properly as designed by God. Man did not just fall to the ground as evidenced by his hiding from God; he also went below the ground to seek life from what God had subjected to death. Every fallen and unregenerated man operates only from the natural realm of life.

The scripture made it clear that those who wander out of the way of understanding shall remain in the congregation of the dead (Proverbs 21:16 NKJV). It is amazing how dead church congregations grow in numbers these days of understanding. Indeed, the congregation of the dead is a reservoir for intellectual wanderers and marauders. Those who litter the streets of purpose are sure to secure permanent memberships in the congregation of the dead. It is sad to note that many homes and marriages of our time are operating from below the ground level due to ignorance.

Some ministries have remained cathedrals of dead souls because they are led by people who have wandered away from understanding to scavenge for survival in the drainage of folly. Many businesses have been ruined simply because their owners prefer the magic wand of instant success to seeking and learning the dynamics of trade and marketing. Rather than invest time in studying and attending seminars, they would be busy visiting magicians and false prophets who have promised them shortcuts to success until they self-destruct.

The coming of Jesus brought salvation and transformation to the fallen man. The regenerate man is one who is raised and is seated with Christ in heavenly places. He's now positioned far above principalities and powers; that, clearly, is indicative of higher ground positioning. This implies that believers have to undergo God's formation process to properly transition into the higher ground.

This inspired book is intended to help believers in Christ Jesus trace their journeys from ground zero to their higher ground, following the lifestyles of men who through practice and obedience exemplified God's formation process.

CHAPTER ONE

The Underground Life

For some, an underground experience may be a training ground. Not everyone who found themselves underground got there by accident and, most likely, not in ignorance or by negligence either. A seed under the ground is not considered buried, but sown into a process of growth. God sows us into this life, expecting us to take deep roots and become fully formed enough to develop strong convictions that can withstand the winds of confusion around us.

For our light and momentary troubles are achieving for us an eternal glory that far outweighs them all. (2 Corinthians 4:17 NIV)

Any affliction, no matter how light, is considered an underground experience. However, the Bible assures us that this is not the end of the story, but just a passing process. You may wonder why suffer affliction in the first place? The simple answer is that affliction is working in line with God's plan for us to produce in us what our carnal nature cannot. An orange needs to be squeezed before its juice comes out. A teabag only releases its flavour when steeped in hot or cold solutions. The path to the far more exceeding and eternal weight of glory leads through a light and momentary underground affliction. We need to endure the momentary affliction in order to enjoy the eternal glory. The first man had to be formed from the dust of the ground before he received the breath of God to become a living soul.

Joseph's Underground Experience

THE PIT:

And they took him, and cast him into a pit: and the pit was empty, there was no water in it. (Genesis 37:24 NKJV)

Most people are familiar with the story of Joseph, the dreamer. He was a young man who, from his teenage years, knew where he was headed in life. Apart from enjoying a unique measure of favour with his father, he was also upright and honest enough to report the evil deeds of his wayward brothers to Jacob. Stepping on some people's toes can often be costly. Joseph bruised his jealous brothers' egos and they repaid him with affliction; but their evil agenda only lasted for a moment in time!

THEY TOOK HIM:

Joseph's brothers denied him one of his most basic fundamental human rights and that is; his freedom of movement. His underground experience began with being exposed to inhumane limitations, hatred, and the ego of his siblings. Their evil act of selling him into slavery made him a victim of unhealthy competition, abnormal traditions, repugnant cultures, and more. He was robbed of the joy of childhood and the privilege of education. There are great men today whose dreams were hijacked early in life by the same people who were supposed to help in promoting and fulfilling such dreams. They only became great later in life due to divine intervention.

Some children were entrusted to the custody of their uncles or aunties who had promised to send them to school in the cities but instead, turned them to menial servants or sold them into the slavery. Others became victims of bad habits through wrong associations and exposure to the evils in their neighbourhoods, which eventually sabotaged their progress in life. There are also those who became victims of wicked, ambitious and insecure bosses in the marketplace. These young, upcoming and vibrant employees are perceived as threats by their superiors who would do everything to frustrate their lives and future. Some uprising ministers have been taken into religious custody by the many so-called spiritual fathers in the Lord whose sole intention is to sabotage the visions and purpose of their protégés.

AND CAST HIM INTO A PIT;

In furthering their evil agenda to eliminate him from a life of societal impact and importance, Joseph's brothers decided to cast him into a pit. The pit signifies a place below the ground level, a place where he would no longer be seen or heard from until he dies. It was a place where death was sure, but slow. They were determined to terminate his dreams by ending his life.

A lot of people are suffering in the pit of obscurity even though they carry greatness on their inside. They've been thrown into the pit of despondency by some "elder brothers" who feared their tenure of wickedness would be terminated if they allow the dreamer among them thrive and succeed.

The good news about the pit, for people who are under a divine mandate, is that it is always empty; void of dangerous animals such as reptiles, scorpions and any other complications that could harm the dream. God in His omniscience arranges it such that, no matter the depth of the pit, it ends up being empty threat.

The same people who cast Joseph into the pit later pulled him out for some other selfish reasons, unbeknownst to them that their plan is still in line with divine agenda. When there was no vehicle or means to take him to his higher ground, they sold him as a slave. Even though he was destined for higher ground, he had to go through the valley of affliction. The way up often requires a downward journey laced with pains and frustrations.

And we know that in all things God works for the good of those who love him, who have been called according to his purpose. (Romans 8:28 NIV)

THE PRISON:

Joseph's master took him and put him in prison, the place where the king's prisoners were confined. But while Joseph was there in the prison, the Lord was with him; he showed him kindness and granted him favour in the eyes of the prison warden. (Genesis 39:20-21, NIV)

It is interesting to note that those who sent Joseph underground were people he was supposed to look up to, yet they also turned out to be the ones he later helped in life. His father sent him to seek after his brother's welfare, but they turned around to harm him instead. His rejection of the lustful advances of Potiphar's wife got him in trouble and landed him in the dungeon. Joseph found himself underground for simply wanting to preserve his master's marriage and refusing to defile his bed. Sometimes, following the path of purpose can be laced with setbacks, but God's faithfulness always sees us through to the end.

Joseph was alone and had no companion in the pit, however, in the dungeon he was able to interact with fellow prisoners even though it was a place of bondage. Often, the first test of genuine ministry is the ability to keep pressing on even when things seem to be going on a downward spiral.

Examples can be made of people who used to be rich but are now broke, people who used to be free who are now bound, people who once are considered royalty but are now prisoners, people who had a glorious past but are now struggling with a helpless present.

The underground is a place where the people around you may be laden with problems and subdued financially, emotionally and physically, just like the prisoners and slaves of ancient kings! The difference between Joseph and other prisoners' circumstances is that, even though their physical and emotional situations seemed similar, their spiritual conditions were different. In Joseph's case, we're told that the Lord was with him and that makes all the difference. It is wonderful to know that God never leaves His own even when they're underground. This is simply because God makes our trying situations work to our advantage. He also gave Joseph the supernatural aid of mercy and favour, even though that did not immediately result in a visible change in his incarceration, yet the effect was tangible. While some were afflicted with sicknesses and diseases in the prison, God's mercy preserved Joseph. While others were subject to hard labour, Joseph enjoyed preferential treatment.

Whenever we find ourselves underground on our journey to greatness, we must not give into despair but remember that the Lord is ever with us. He will shield us with mercy and we shall surely find favour with men through the trying moments.

Are you oppressed by masters who themselves are limited in purpose and impact? Don't lose courage because it's a sign that you're on your way to the higher ground.

No test or temptation that comes your way is beyond the course of what others have had to face. All you need to remember is that God will never let you down; he'll never let you be pushed past your limit; he'll always be there to help you come through it. (1 Corinthians 10:13, MSG)

Jonah's Underground

Even though Jonah landed underground for a wrong reason, he, however, became a perfect of example of God's redeeming power from self-inflicted pitfalls. Some people's afflictions are self-inflicted so they spiral into a lifecycle that is way below God's plan for them. These sad realities notwithstanding, God is too faithful to abandon them to the consequences of their errors, no matter how deep into the underground they fell.

Disobedience is a quick route to the underground as illustrated in the life of Jonah. To walk in contradiction to God's purpose, counsel and instructions, is to purchase an express ticket to the underground. One may appear to be on a fast and smooth journey, but the end is usually almost certain to end in pain and disappointment.

HE ROSE UP:

But Jonah rose up to flee unto Tarshish from the presence of the Lord, and went down to Joppa; and he found a ship going to Tarshish: so he paid the fare thereof, and went down into it, to go with them unto Tarshish from the presence of the Lord. (Jonah 1:3 NKJV)

Jonah's journey to the underground began with him first rising up. It's almost as if one rises only to proceed on a journey towards falling. Many today are elevated in resources and gadgets but they also are setting themselves up for a fall. People who used to learn memory verses through printed Bibles are now leaning on handy electronic Bibles for easy search results options that come in handy for quick results.

Jonah rose to flee. He didn't rise to the occasion and his responsibilities as ordained by God. Some people will put in extra hours for more pay under the pretense of raising funds for the Lord. They would promise their pastors support for kingdom projects once these funds come into their possession. Unfortunately, it is only a matter of time before such people are exposed as fleeing from responsibilities and accountability in the house of God. Some brethren have abandoned their duties in the church in pursuit of political power only to realize later that they are fleeing from the presence of God. Most of the rising trends that people covertly commit themselves to are not for edification, but an escape route from obedience.

DOWN TO JOPPA:

Joppa could be identified in Jonah's case as the connecting point to his main place of rebellion. It is where the transport to his carnal destination is found. People hardly go straight from living Scripture-based lives to living riotous ones. No, they tend to first connect with old friends, often at work or in business where they can easily find excuses and yield to their weaknesses by boarding the sinful ship sailing to their carnal desires. Joppa is midway from the place of instruction to the place of destruction. Where is your Joppa? That place where you always find a ship that ferries you away from focus, fervency and faith? Where is Joppa in your life? A place where you always go to before coming home to your spouse?

Look, there is always a ship at Joppa, manned and ready to carry you to fulfill your lustful desires, teaching you deceptions and scheming you out of God's plan and purpose. There is a ship at Joppa which is positioned by the world and the devil to carry you into adultery, compromise, stealing, masturbation and other evils. Such ships are never going to Nineveh where your assignment is, but to Tarshish where your desires are. Those who go underground, go astray and easily find a means to get there. While those heading for fulfillment in ministry and marriage may wait a while before finding the right ship. Those going away from the will of God always have a ready ride to their regrets.

PAYING THE FARE:

The way below always attracts a fee in life. You cannot ride for free against the purpose of God. You will pay a heavy price for it. Some have paid with a good marriage; some have paid the price of a promising ministry, and others have paid with their health and friends. There are those who paid the ultimate price; their lives. A lot of people are paying dearly for things without reward and for journeys without results.

Have you used the resources that are meant to fulfill the heavenly mandate for your life in Nineveh, to pay for personal ambition? One of the greatest threats to missionary work today is that people misuse mission funds to live a life of luxury. If we divert resources that are meant for supporting and promoting the kingdom mandate to other things, we are investing in the underground trip. After payment, Jonah went down into it. He was swallowed by it. Where you invest is where you will get into. If you're getting down into the wrong relationship with lust, stop investing in it. It is what you pay for that gives you a pass to its core.

Stop paying attention, time and resources to wrong relationships. Before you know it, you're already going down into being forgotten.

GOING WITH THEM:

The big ship of disobedience has plenty of travelers along its carnal routes. You may not have people who would willingly follow you to the Nineveh of obedience, but there are unsolicited companions who love to be around you in disobedience. It is common to find ministers going with the trends rather than going with the truth; going with men rather than going with God. Who are you going with in life? Who do you find it easy to flow with?

Wide is the gate and broad is the way that leads to destruction, and there are many who go in by it. (Matthew 7:13 NKJV)

One of the fastest ways to go underground is to decide to travel "with them": to be on the entourage of the majority and choose popular opinion in contrast to the purpose of God. There are believers who are leaving truthful Christian foundations where the principles of Christ are taught and enforced, to follow "them" where anything goes. It got worse for Jonah along the way. You may begin the journey of disobedience peacefully, but it cannot end in peace. There is a storm of correction that beats against wrong relationships and you cannot survive it because God is not involved. It may look like you can afford the journey initially, but you would later discover that your means cannot cover the cost.

Then the Lord sent a great wind on the sea, and such a violent storm arose that the ship threatened to break up. (Jonah 1:4 NIV)

Rebellion does not end with your actions; it attracts a divine reaction. God will react sooner or later. Stubborn people live under the illusion that rascality begins and ends with them. Armed robbers usually believe they are smart enough to avoid detection and that all roads lead to riches. However, many of them are shocked when they are caught and wonder how investigations uncovered them. If human detectives can nab illegal offenders, how could a man assume that he can escape from the long everlasting Arms of God if he runs away from purpose? We usually bind the devil and ascribe storms to devilish attacks. However, the sender of this great wind in Jonah's life was the Lord himself.

Now, if the Lord sends a great wind against your life, do you have a scientific windshield to prevent its effects? Before the ship breaks into pieces, would you own up and confess your disobedience? After Jonah's confession to the people, the Lord who sent a great wind had also prepared a great fish to swallow up Jonah.

Now the Lord provided a huge fish to swallow Jonah, and Jonah was in the belly of the fish three days and three nights. (Jonah 1:17 NIV)

God's got you covered no matter how deeply you've sunk into disobedience. God has his prepared agents at every point and place. Confession may bring us into temporary confinement but it will deliver us to eventual fulfillment. God gets involved the moment your heart gets resolved to follow Him.

Underground For 38 Years

One who was there had been an invalid for thirty-eight years. When Jesus saw him lying there and learned that he had been in this condition for a long time, he asked him, "Do you want to get well?" "Sir," the invalid replied, "I have no one to help me into the pool when the water is stirred. While I am trying to get in, someone else goes down ahead of me." (John 5:5-7 NIV)

The place this man was found was around a marketplace pool that was meant for impotent folks. It was a place for people whose potentials had been impaired by sicknesses or natural disasters. This underground state of life was not curable and he was too broke to afford anything. This had lasted for thirty eight years of his life! It is not everyone underground that got there by disobedience or because of trials of faith. Some find themselves there due to some natural disadvantages. Some were born impotent in the brain or in the body.

The beauty of this man's example is that his condition didn't stop Jesus from seeing or getting to him. We may be hindered from going upward or forward, from seeing the right people or knowing the right people, by certain disadvantages in life, but those disabilities will not disable Jesus from seeing us. Jesus saw him as he lay there. He couldn't even rise to be noticed, but right where he was lying, Jesus saw him.

Jesus also knew that this case had lasted a long time. Sometimes, we stay for so long underground and conclude over time that Jesus doesn't know how long we have battled with the challenges. We get so used to old issues that we no longer discuss them with new people in our lives or even with God. Jesus knows how long you have stayed single and not married. He knows how long you have been unemployed and out of a job. He knows how long you have been married without a baby, how long you have been in ministry without helpers. No matter your underground, you're not just known by God, He also has an update concerning your situation.

Most times, the tragedy is that we get so used to our conditions and limitations that we lose sense of ever being made whole. Over time, we tend to delete the possibilities of recovery and wholeness. Being underground conditions our expectations to what has happened and shuts us off to what can happen—what the possibilities are. No man can walk if he has a lame will.

A story was told of an aged man who was lame for over four decades. He was brought on a wheelchair by his grandchildren in faith to a crusade ground for healing. During the meeting, miracles began to happen and lame folks were instructed to stand up in faith and walk. Ushers and caregivers assisted many by faith to walk and they indeed received their miracles. When they noticed that the old man was still seated, the ushers challenged his grandchildren for being slack in helping the man up. Their response shocked the ushers. The man declined help because he claimed his incapacity had lasted for so many years and started even before the pastor praying for him was born! He went home as the only lame man without healing.

Do You Want To Get Well?

Considering the reality that you have been abandoned by friends and family and left to wallow in bitterness for a long time, do you still preserve the willingness to be made whole? Realizing that no one has been there for you through the struggles of life in the underground, is your hope to be made whole still alive? Do you still desire that your life be put together to make a whole number? It is difficult and rare to spend almost four decades underground and yet have a higher ground response to challenging questions about wholeness.

The man in our scripture was full of complaints about being alone in his struggles. People throw a lot of pity parties by indicting others for abandoning them in their difficulty. Instead of focusing on the future and being ready in the present, they rehearse the past. Underground mentality has details about, what is not working, being disadvantaged, and being behind in stepping into the healing pool of possibilities. Sadly, most of his excuses were real and genuine. He said: "...while I am trying to get in, someone else goes down ahead of me." Sometimes, we find ourselves lagging behind financially, in ministry or business while others overtake us to breast the tape of success. It is akin to saying, "I make efforts to get better, but while I try, others walk ahead of me." How can you overtake natural sprinters when you're confined by nature to lag behind?

However, that was not the right response to the question. He had been subdued by pessimism over the years; he had built his mindset on negative facts and couldn't learn the lyrics of faith again. Living underground is living on the facts of life: living on higher ground is living by faith on the Word of God. Faith needs no support from the negative facts of the past, no matter how real they seem. Faith is not an inference drawn from years of observation, but a conclusion by revelation. Higher ground is responding to life's questions by faith, rising and taking up your bed of weaknesses and pronto, you begin to walk! You may never walk until you rise up from your past orientations. You need to take up the bed as a testimony to others of where you have been.

CHAPTER TWO

The Level Ground

For believers, the Cross of Jesus is a leveler. The vilest offender who truly believes, that moment from Jesus a pardon receives! It is where a new page was opened for us to write a fresh story of grace. As a young boy, my son came to me with a composition or essay he was writing. He had made some mistakes while putting pen to paper and had to cancel out many things due to wrong spellings or incorrect arrangement of thoughts. After writing, the page became practically illegible. He was hesitant and apprehensive as he brought the defaced page to me with the many mistakes. I just smiled, tore out a fresh sheet of paper for him to rewrite the composition.

He returned with a neater note.

There is a new sheet of paper at the Cross for you to re- write your story, no matter how badly you've defaced the initial and previous opportunities. You only need to bring your past scribbled pages to the blood-filled fountain and be washed therein. The Cross is the platform where the feet of the ladder to greatness rests with eternal realities.

The teachers of the law and the Pharisees brought in a woman caught in adultery. They made her stand before the group 4 and said to Jesus, "Teacher, this woman was caught in the act of adultery." (John 8:3-4 NIV)

The intention for bringing the woman to Jesus was to accuse Jesus and ridicule the woman. The accusers didn't know they were securing the woman's life with eternal insurance. Grace turns things that are designed to hurt you into things that bring you favour. Whatever takes you to Jesus is an escalator of grace, no matter how ill-intentioned and crazily designed it may appear. They gave "the very act" description of her underground life in order to eliminate her probability for pardon and passage to the higher ground. But no gravity can pull you down from the grip of grace! There is no information of accusation that can reduce your chances for forgiveness.

"...Then neither do I condemn you," Jesus declared. "Go now and leave your life of sin." (John 8:11 NIV)

Condemnation defeats liberation. To go forward and onward in life, you need to start by getting a pardon from Jesus. The release came with a tone of freedom: GO! She came bound but left free. She was seized in iniquity but redeemed in victory. If Jesus sets you free, you're free indeed. The Cross is the launchpad for progress in life where you can receive the license to go higher without the weight of condemnation. The woman was brought tied with the rope of accusation and released in the hope of freedom. To keep the momentum, she had a responsibility: sin no more!

You cannot keep repeating your past and think you could be releasing your future. Higher ground requires a divorce from what held you back and involves tying the knot with Jesus who sets you free. There are things in your life that shouldn't continue if you want to climb up. There are attitudes you must drop, mentalities and addictions that cannot be part of your future. She could no longer go back to the guy she was committing adultery with.

Who needs to be stricken off your contact list? Who needs to be excommunicated from your circle of influence? Who brought you into the current mess you're in and has left you to suffer alone? They need to be deleted from your album of friendship! Who do you have to stop seeing? Where do you have to stop going to? What things do you have to stop saying? To come up to the higher ground, change is not only inevitable, it is mandatory.

Shave and Change

...and he shaved himself, and changed his raiment, and came in unto Pharaoh. (Genesis 41:9-14 KJV)

Shaving is required to trim off excess hair, especially beards. Likewise, there are excesses that must be shaved off to attain the level ground in readiness for the higher ground. Joseph shaved himself: this means that nobody will do it for you. Level ground demands personal responsibility and adjustment to the next phase of your growth. What are the things growing in your life that need to be shaved off? For some people, they need to shave off their greed, anger, excessive talking, negative attitude, etc. Hair, when properly trimmed, can enhance good looks, but becomes wild and unsightly if left untrimmed.

Anything left to itself without a check grows wild. A wild life is a lifestyle that is not under control. There are people who live a life of outrageous excesses. Not necessarily the canonical sins, but human indecencies—all for a change of status. This is not about what is alien to a person, but what he is by nature. You cannot just leave your life to natural tendencies and human inclinations. You should know when to 'grab that razor' and put a check on certain things in your life. You should know when to stop negative imaginations in your sexual and mental life, and bring every thought to obedience in Christ.

Joseph also changed his raiment, his clothes. Not washed, not mended, not ironed, but changed his raiment. You don't wear prison clothes to the higher ground. To establish your readiness for the next level, you must change certain imprisoning garments that are characteristic of your current identity. The prison garment is an underground means of identification, with a tag of reproach. You cannot carry an imprisoned mentality to freedom. The prison garment could be people who reduce your thoughts and freedom to their parochial bias and sentimental inclinations. You cannot wash those garments or straighten them with a pressing iron of explanations. You just have to change them. They cannot step out with you into the next phase of your life. Do you have the courage to unbutton those prison garments and put on Christ's liberty?

A friend narrated how he was dressing his four year old son some time ago. While he dressed his son, the mother called out the boy from the other side of their apartment. The child did not respond to his mother. Angrily, she dashed into the room where the father and son were and lashed out at the boy for ignoring her call. "Did you not hear that I was calling you?" the mother wondered. The boy responded with, "Sorry mum, but daddy was getting me dressed!" It was obvious to her that her son couldn't respond while being dressed up. There are calls in your life that must wait until you're fully dressed. There are places you cannot go if you're dressed inappropriately. Change your raiment of expression: a smile is the best costume, integrity is the best perfume. Dress yourself with humility and get rid of the arrogant jacket that imprisoned you and prevented you from learning. Wear simplicity of disposition in your relationships and get rid of complicated attires. Put on the whole armour of God so you can withstand the compromise of the evil days and having done all to stand.

Joseph was not brought in to Pharaoh until he worked on himself. He could not access the throne until he adjusted to the palace standards. The standards of the place you're coming from might not admit you to the place you're going to. You must learn the new standard in order to have the right template that can access the future. When you successfully achieve personal growth and development, you have set yourself up on a level ground, ready and booked for the next flight to the higher ground.

Salvation On The Cross

But the other criminal rebuked him. "Don't you fear God," he said, "since you are under the same sentence? We are punished justly, for we are getting what our deeds deserve. But this man has done nothing wrong." Then he said, "Jesus, remember me when you come into your kingdom." Jesus answered him, "Truly I tell you, today you will be with me in paradise." (Luke 23:40-43, NIV)

Be The Other Man

At the cross, two malefactors were given the privilege of meeting Jesus by providence and given the opportunity to cross to the level ground. One was railing at Jesus like the religious people and the accusers, but the other man chose to be different. He rebuked the railing guy. He sided with Jesus and opposed his mate.

Coming to the level ground at the cross is to testify against the world. It is to defend the truth and the sacrifice of Jesus on the Cross. It is easy for many people to remain quiet in order not to be castigated by their partners in crime and therefore, they sheepishly follow the wrong train to doom. Many people have ruined themselves because the leading voices around them refused to acknowledge the Lordship of Jesus and they wanted to belong to the circle of socialites.

Some ladies are aware that sleeping around in amorous relationships is a heinous sin against their bodies and God, but they lack the courage to say so to friends in the same trade in order not to be blacklisted by them. It is time to step out of the destructive and doomed sinful network and embrace Christ and His cross. Be the other man in your office and neighbourhood who will embrace Jesus and appreciate his sacrifice. Be the other lady to step out of compromising contracts that nail your conscience to the cross; embrace the offer of grace before you find yourself crossing over to eternal condemnation.

Do not allow associations to deprive you of salvation. The level ground is a personal territory consequent upon an individual decision. There is no mass ticket to Jesus but an individual and personal repentance and conversion.

Do You Fear God?

One trait in the "other man" was the fear of God. He challenged the adamant malefactor to fear God. You cannot experience the level ground if you denounce the Lordship of Jesus and the supremacy of God. "The fear of the Lord is the beginning of wisdom, and knowledge of the Holy

One is understanding" (Proverbs 9:10, NIV). No matter how smart you think of yourself, how highly rated academically or socially, the foundation of wisdom is the fear of the Lord. If a man does not fear the Lord, he has no beginning for living wisely; he has nothing to offer in union with understanding life. Knowing the Holy One means coming to acknowledge a life of holiness and purity opens up your understanding to how you can be guided through life. You cannot make holy decisions or live a holy life if you do not regard God with reverence. If you fear the Lord as mighty and terrible, as the Judge of the whole universe and the Creator who holds your life, then, you wouldn't be cheating on your wife, cracking jokes with unholy things, stealing from others, falsifying figures at work or plotting another person's downfall.

Fearing God emboldens you to confront compromise and resist the temptation to be bought over. Fearing God helps you get convicted to see your true sinful state. It exposes you to the hope of redemption. Fearing man ensnares you to condemnation, but fearing God opens you to justification. "Now all has been heard; here is the conclusion of the matter. Fear God and keep his commandment, for this is the duty of all mankind" (Ecclesiastes 12:13, NIV).

Have you recognized fearing God as a duty? It is not an optional or volunteer obligation, but a mandatory duty! The repentant malefactor was objective about the consequences of his action and properly expressed that the condemnation passed on them was justifiable. He had no good reason for doing the bad things he did. That is a man entering the level ground with the fear of God. He was not trying to see others as more condemnable while he had a load of guilt heaped at his doorstep.

Remember Me

This refers to remembering who he has become and not what he did wrong or where he came from. Confessing and admitting faults puts you in the diary of forgiveness with God. An adamant sinner is wasted and forgotten. The repentant criminal was not pardoned from dying on the cross, but he was pardoned from being wiped off from eternal memory. The way to be reconciled with God is to come pleading and not bragging. The old saying goes: the shortest pencil is better than the longest memory. There is a book of life where names of saints are documented for remembrance. "Anyone whose name was not found written in the book of life was thrown into the lake of fire" (Revelation 20:15, NIV).

Eternity will be divided between the book of life and the lake of fire. One is a documented repository of the faithful and the other is the eternal garbage for the sinful. There is one thing that will be done with everybody's name; all names will be searched. The search result will depend on whether a man's name was written or not. You cannot smuggle names into the book until you make a subscription by faith for salvation. It should not shock anyone to note that the decision to cast into the lake of fire is binding on WHOSOEVER! Whether a man had money or fame on earth or not, was tall or short, black or white, educated or illiterate, bishop or layman, known or hidden: whosoever not found, would be cast into the lake of fire! Would your name be found written if a search is conducted today?

Today In Paradise

Your admission into the family of God does not require special protocol or bureaucratic approval that may take weeks or days before your visa is decided. Jesus responded with an instant grant and a true promise! It was immediate for a man punished for a capital offence and the mode for anyone is not different. The door is open today but tomorrow may be too late.

CHAPTER THREE

The Higher Ground

Salvation is God's gift to man, fulfilling purpose is man's gift to God. Isn't it honourable to present a gift to God in eternity? Salvation is not an end in itself but a means to an end. You were not saved in order to brandish the salvation badge or brag in tongues; there is a purpose that a man cannot fulfill except he is reconciled to God. Jesus died so that man can be restored to the purpose for his living. That is the higher ground spiritually.

In the Lord, the sky is not our limit. There is always room to move higher. You can move from one level of glory to the other. There are many levels of glory. We have the glory of the stars, the sun, moon, celestial bodies and bodies terrestrial.

There are also heavenly bodies and there are earthly bodies; but the splendor of the heavenly bodies is one kind, and the splendor of the earthly bodies is another. "The sun has one kind of splendour, the moon another and the stars another; and star differs from star in splendour. (1 Corinthians 15:40-41, NIV)

The plan of God is to move us from one higher ground to the other. So you can never stop longing, yearning, desiring, and praying for the higher ground.

The path of the righteous is like the morning sun, shining ever brighter till the full light of day. Proverbs 4:18 (NIV)

Many are stuck at a lower ground because of their carelessness, and laziness in aspiring and praying to God for higher ground. I pray that it will not be written on your epitaph that you remained at a certain level because you failed to ask.

You do not have because you do not ask God. (James 4:2, NIV)

For Jonah, he cried to God from his ground zero and God heard him. The Lord gave Jonah a second chance and he started hearing God's word again. His higher ground came about when he was restored fully to God. His higher ground was when he started to obey God and enjoy a deeper communion with God.

Then the word of the Lord came to Jonah a second time... (Jonah 3:1, NIV)

The Word of God came to Jonah again. God's Word is powerful and impactful. Jonah was empowered and he became an enviable envoy for God. He delivered the Word of God without any form of compromise.

Joseph's higher ground was when he was lifted to the exalted position of a Prime Minister in Egypt.

Then Pharaoh said to his officials, "Isn't this the man we need? Are we going to find anyone else who has God's spirit in him like this?" So Pharaoh said to Joseph, "You're the man for us. God has given you the inside story—no one is as qualified as you in experience and wisdom. From now on, you're in charge of my affairs; all my people will report to you. Only as king will I be over you." So Pharaoh commissioned Joseph: "I'm putting you in charge of the entire country of Egypt." Then Pharaoh removed his signet ring from his finger and slipped it on Joseph's hand. He outfitted him in robes of the best linen and put a gold chain around his neck. He put the second-in-command chariot at his disposal, and as he rode people shouted "Bravo!" Joseph was in charge of the entire country of Egypt. (Genesis 41:38-43, MSG)

Waiting Lane

"But those who hope in the Lord will renew their strength. They will soar on wings like eagles; they will run and not grow weary, they will walk and not be faint." (Isaiah 40:31, NIV)

Gaining height is a process linked to a promise. Some people gain stability with the promise of God, but stagger in the process. The difference between those who gain the height in destiny and those who drop is not the prophetic promise, but the process. It is not all who hear the promise that attain it, but those who wait for it. The hopeful wait is the sure connection to higher ground. The Bible differentiates the higher ground from other grounds with the waiting clause, but what makes the waiting worthwhile is who they wait on.

You cannot get to higher ground on a solo run. Who you believe in determines your end. Hope is a fruit, but it may be sour or sweet depending on whom you place your hope in. Patience is a virtue, but it may attract value or it may not, depending on whom you're waiting on. Higher ground is not a hurried life project but a steady process to an irreversible development. Strength is basic to mounting up and such strength is built up by constant contact with the source of all strength—God. The force is determined by the source! Many people are on the journey to higher ground but won't make it up eventually because they depend on their own strength or on other people's strength.

The life that mounts up is a strong life that lives by renewal. You cannot use the old strength for a new height. You cannot know only what you knew in the past and expect to do what you ought to do in the future. Throughout the life of an eagle, there are changes to the colours of its eyes, beak, feathers and claws, indicating stages of growth and development and consequently, stronger adaptation. The eagle does not die with the feathers it was born with. Between birth and death are a series of responsibilities and demands that require stronger features. The feathers at birth cannot soar but depend solely on the flying capacity of the mother eagle. However, a point comes when the young eagle would have to fly for itself.

Many Christian's lives don't progress as they should because they don't renew their strength: they depend on the strength of yesterday for their tomorrow. The key to a new height is new strength; we cannot do better than we know. Many people feed on stale bread in life and expect to grow into new health. How will that happen? The eagle needs to grow new claws to replace the young, weak ones if it intends to survive. There are intellectual claws that must be grown and developed to have a firm grip on preys of profit, lest they slip off. We cannot hold on to young claws and feed the adult need. Paul the apostle puts it more succinctly: "When I was a child, I talked like a child; I thought like a child, I reasoned like a child. When I became a man, I put the ways of childhood behind me" (I Corinthians 13:11, NIV).

Paul showed three things that are typical with children and which must be renewed and replaced as we grow into the higher ground of development. He gave a demarcating tense about his life process: "when I was" a child. You can only notice change when you have grown. If there is no notable change in your growth processes, you're dying and headed nowhere. Were you a child in your past? or after so many years, are you still a child? It is not about adding up in age and celebrating decades of birthdays, it is about changing in your speaking, understanding and thought pattern.

Speaking As A Child

A child's speech is not always coherent or clear hence, they tend to find communication difficult and, where there is communication difficultly, the communicator is usually misunderstood and consequently often mistreated or placated with what they don't actually need. Some children would cry out so loud and with so much pain out of frustration and these often develop into pent-up aggression in them as they become older age.

More importantly, young children speak mostly gibberish. They speak three things: fear, food and fun. Fear of bugs: flies, cockroaches, insects, etc. As an adult, you wonder how children look so big and yet get easily scared by things not even as big as their toes. However, there are sixty-year-olds today who still flee from cockroaches and this is probably simply because they're yet to renew their strength.

Food: most of the interesting conversations children have with their parents' center around food. They sleep and play around until they get driven by hunger. They learn names of their favourite foods before being able to pronounce their own names. There are also people who, even at fifty, only get excited about food. Children don't know when or where to ask for food.

When my son was a toddler, we were in a church gathering one day. It was an intense prayer meeting and he was hungry. He just found his way to the podium and tapped me before the ushers could pick him up. I leaned over in shock to see him and he whispered something I couldn't decipher. So I stooped low to listen. "Daddy, I want plantain chips," was his request; right in the middle of a mountain-moving prayer meeting! That's a child for you. Children talk more than they think. They largely repeat what they hear, and not what they think. Most times, this puts them in trouble with adults who punish them for being loose with their mouths.

There is a way you talk and expose your ignorance or prevent your deliverance from captivity. It was the way Abigail spoke that softened the heart of David and prevented bloodshed in her household, and she eventually became the wife of the king. There are utterances that prevent people from ascending to their prepared places. Many people have been ensnared by their own words.

The words of the reckless pierce like swords, but the tongue of the wise brings healing. (Proverbs12:18, NIV)

Evildoers are trapped by their sinful talk, and so the innocent escape trouble. (Proverbs 12: 13, NIV)

Many homes are not getting into higher ground emotionally because of the words coming out of the spouses to themselves and to their children. Many ministries are stunted in growth because they are fed with childish milk of God's Word and not the meat. Many companies have become moribund because of wrong attitudes and answers by the bosses to important subjects. Many governments have been brought down because the heads of such governments gave childish responses to mature questions. Some have been defeated and afflicted by the devil because they do not have the scriptural responses to the challenges of demons. They are not rich in the will and Word of God. They do not see the Word as a sword of the Spirit to avenge all disobedience against the truth of righteousness. To get to the higher ground, we must speak faith as adults, speak the truth as mature people and speak life as spiritual beings. Jesus said: "...The words I have spoken to you—they are full of the Spirit and life" (John 6: 63, NIV).

Understanding As A Child

Understanding enhances success in the journey to higher ground. The understanding of a child is shallow and superficial. Higher ground demands a deeper understanding. Children understand basic rules and rudimentary principles which should generally suffice for some particular stage of growing up. However, once a child grows into adulthood, life's questions become more complicated and sophisticated thus requiring great understanding to put the puzzles together. This analogy brings to mind the story of a woman as narrated to me by a friend. This lady was reported to have wanted a baked cake so badly that she prayed fervently to God for it. In response, God sent several people to her with supplies of different baking ingredients such as oil, butter, eggs, sugar, and flour. These people carried out God's instruction without knowing or questioning why He asked them to provide these items to this woman.

After a while, this woman began to rail at God for sending her all these ingredients she never asked for because her simple request to Him was for a baked cake. God, in His patience, sent another person to tell her that He has, as a matter of fact, answered her request for a cake several weeks ago. When she heard this, she wondered how that was possible. God's response through His messenger was, "I sent you all the ingredients you need to bake your cake, but you seem to lack the necessary understanding to put them together!"

Understanding helps you to move from the cry for cake to bringing the ingredients of God's provision together and bake a message out of the mess. Many people have been given success disguised in the garment of hard work, but they do not consider it because they possess the understanding of a child. Understanding gives you the ability to hear what is unspoken and to see what is hidden from the eyes so that you can do what may seem impossible to the ordinary mind.

Babies only understand how to put things in their mouths and to suck milk from their mother's breasts. Also, they only know how to damage things and not how to keep or preserve them. All they understand is eat, sleep and wake up for more food. Some people can narrate a movie and understand it from beginning to end, but they do not understand Scripture. Some people understand fashion but see spiritual passion as a riddle. Some know how to throw parties, but can't fathom how a mission or a ministry works. They understand science but are ignorant of the Scriptures. They understand miracles, but not the principles of God's words.

When anyone hears the message about the kingdom and does not understand it, the evil one comes and snatches away what was sown in their heart. (Matthew 13:19, NIV)

Imagine the tragedy of a life that does not understand as it ought. It is alarming to see that the word of the kingdom could be heard but not understood. It is not because it is a complex message, but because the hearers have shut their hearts to understanding. A man can open his eyes during a sermon, open his ears for exhortations and yet close his heart from understanding them. Lack of understanding is a deficiency of the heart which paralyzes possibilities in a man. Where understanding is lacking, there is an invitation to the wicked one to cart away what was sown in the heart. There is a depletion and robbery of the heart that does not understand the Word of the kingdom. The reason many are not fruitful today is because the truth about growth that has been sown into them is shut out of their meditation and so cannot produce understanding. Thus, the wicked one takes advantage of their ignorance.

Do You Understand What You Are Reading?

Then Philip ran up to the chariot and heard the man reading Isaiah the prophet. "Do you understand what you are reading?" Philip asked. "How can I," he said, "unless someone explains it to me?" So he invited Philip to come up and sit with him." (Act 8:30-31, NIV)

As an undergraduate, there were students in class who were referred to as trees of books but were fruitless in grades. They read till day broke (TDB), always in the class but never getting good results. Many of them had the lowest grades in the class. They spent a large quantity of time but did not have quality study. It is possible to be devoted religiously to what one does and yet be without understanding while continuing in it. Some people would prefer being religiously correct even if it negates scriptural reasoning. There are several people on the pulpit today carrying out denominational agendas that they cannot scripturally explain themselves. They are just doing it for show and not for impact.

One of the ways to escape the entanglement of shallow understanding is to embrace God's guiding lights around us. These are people who have the right spiritual exposure to the truth and are visibly living by it. We benefit from them when we are open and truthful in admitting our limited understanding of scriptural realities. We must admit the need for a guide, regardless of our political, social and financial status. Understanding is enhanced by the readiness to learn and be guided into all truth.

Like the Eunuch, we must also desire to hold ministers with accurate and truthful insight to the word of God in high esteem, and make them comfortable in discharging their spiritual responsibilities. We should give them an 'up' honour and seated comfort. "How can I," he said, "unless someone explains it to me?" So he invited Philip to come up and sit with him." (Act 8:31, NIV). Some rich people live shallow lives because of how lowly they esteem the ministers who could help them to reach clear perspectives of God's word. Honouring such ministers is important if we intend to cast away childish understanding.

Thinking As A Child

The peculiarity about a child's thought is not how they think, but what they think about. Children think about the present and not the future, they think of themselves and not others, they think about what they want and not about what it costs. Children think about what to get and not what to give. They think about playing and not praying. They think about what they see others do and not on what they should do. They think on what someone said, not on what is true. These thoughts will get you nowhere near to higher ground. Higher ground involves selfless thoughts that incubate vision in the womb of value. The Scripture gives a prescription on what mature thoughts look like:

Finally, brothers and sisters, whatever is true, whatever is noble, whatever is right, whatever is pure, whatever is lovely, whatever is admirable— if anything is excellent or praiseworthy—think about such things. (Philippians 4:8, NIV)

The above is the basis of higher ground thought. These are thoughts that take men to the top and sustain them there. A man's value is the worth of his thoughts. The strength of matured minds is the ability to keep the slippery mind within the confines of acceptable thoughts. Those are thoughts that prove a child has become a man spiritually. The hardest part of conversion is in the thought region. Jesus placed much emphasis on shaping the thoughts of his disciples regarding many issues before they fully grasped His message. He couldn't take them beyond where their thoughts allowed.

For instance, He changed their thoughts on prayer: "And when you pray, do not keep on babbling like pagans, for they think they will be heard because of their many words" (Matthew 6:7, NIV). Many Christians boast today about how long they spend praying in order to impress struggling Christians and position themselves as prayer warriors. Jesus made an attempt to change that thought in his days and pointed out that long prayers with continuous babbling was not a spiritual emblem but an identity of the heathens. They say so much, thinking, not really knowing, that they will be heard because of their many words.

Have you heard how loudly and repeatedly some people shout the name of Jesus—maybe seven times— before praying? Can you imagine your child as a father, calling you seven times on every occasion he intends to discuss something with you? Do you know why some prayer warriors ask others to do so? Well, If God doesn't hear the first time, he will by the second or third or fourth and definitely before the seventh! How far has Jesus changed our thinking on this in the modern church? No wonder we hold several vigils and nothing spiritual is awake in us. Thinking a long prayer is an effective prayer does not portray spiritual maturity fit for the higher ground experience.

Jesus also warns against anxious thought: "Therefore I tell you, do not worry about your life, what you will eat or drink; or about your body, what you will wear. Is not life more than food and the body more than clothes?" (Matthew 6:25, NIV)

How many hours in a day do we invest thinking about what to eat, drink or wear? Many people go late to church, particularly on Sundays, because they waste a lot of time thinking about what to wear. Some people falsify figures in order to unjustly enrich themselves because of selfish desires and thoughts about what to eat, drink or wear. Anxiety is an enemy of faith. Jesus wants us to depend on Him for our daily bread, without worrying about how He's going to fix the future.

One of the ways to overcome anxious thoughts is to attempt objective and sincere answers to Jesus's questions: is your life not more than meat? Is your body not more than raiment? These questions require personal responses to judge individually whether you understand that your life is worth more or less than food. Some people are always offended at occasions where they are not given food. They throw away caution and dignity in order to secure a plate of grains. Do you take care of your body spiritually and medically like you invest in raiment? If the word of God doesn't influence your thoughts, it cannot develop you into maturity.

Gaining Ground

Therefore let us move beyond the elementary teachings about Christ and be taken forward to maturity... (Hebrews 6:1, NIV)

To gain higher ground requires constant movement, a progressive motion and a deliberate shift forward. People naturally easily settle for the comfortable and immediate, dwelling around the familiar and fearing the unknown. The elementary cannot generate enough momentum for the ultimate prize. The sums in elementary class do not task the cerebrum and it is easy to score top marks. There are many people who topped their classes in elementary school, breaking records and winning awards but they started declining as they moved up. The elementary class is basic and foundational, but who commissions a house before he has laid the foundation?

The "claim it and have it" teachings are elementary doctrines that place a steel bar on the growth potential of believers since it does not expose men to the diet of process and the trials of faith. The Christian faith preaches the promises of God but that's not all that Christianity stands for. The teaching of faith without the teaching of works is elementary because it produces barren believers who carry dead faith. Unfortunately, men love the motivational more than the spiritual; they love a faith journey that only requires subscription by confession while they watch God perform on a solo run.

Joining the fellowship of brethren is foundational and elementary, but becoming resourceful and impactful is the higher ground that believers must seek in the body of Christ. Many people today prefer joining fellowships without participating in any unit of the workforce to become productive and accountable to the church. They love to be freelance worshippers with the ease of exit at the slightest provocation. The upsurge in crowds trooping to the church today may not translate to fruitful kingdom growth until the saints are thoroughly furnished and equipped beyond the buttered gospel of packaged Christianity.

Our motion can only become a strong movement when we grow beyond the cultural and enter into the Scriptural. Until our teachings and principles are improved to educate saints and transform them into a wholesome breed of believers, the quest for higher ground remains a mirage. We must dig deeper in our Bible Study meetings, beyond narrations and into revelation; we must have richer content rather than mere comments.

In fact, though by this time you ought to be teachers, you need someone to teach you the elementary truths of God's word all over again. You need milk, not solid food! Anyone who lives on milk, being still an infant, is not acquainted with the teaching about righteousness. But solid food is for the mature, who by constant use have trained themselves to distinguish good from evil. (Hebrews 5:12-14, NIV)

Teach You Again?

No man can gain the higher ground by repeating the class. When my son got promoted to Grade 2, he loved his teacher so much that he did not want to leave her class. Upon resumption of a new semester, he insisted that I should take him to his former class. I told him that the only way to become the pilot that he wanted to be was to change his class and move forward. He eventually passed that stage and finished in brilliant colours. He learnt that he needed to face new tasks and even new teachers. Part of learning is to adapt to new teachers. You don't select who your teacher should be in school. It is the duty of the school management to determine who best fits into a particular class and you have no choice than to get used to that.

In learning however, it will be alarming if a younger person with homework from your previous class asks for help and you as the senior still needs the teacher to teach you again before you can help!

Some Christians do not internalize the lessons of faith or personalize them. They only cram them in their heads and teach others from head knowledge. Yet it should be part of their principles of life. You will be shocked to see that when these Christians need to make decisions based on what they have learned and even taught others, they would act like they have no idea about what the Scripture says on such issues. It is even some of the people that they have taught that will have to teach them again.

Becoming Milk Feeders

What are you becoming in the church despite years of attending Sunday school and seminary? A Christian who is not applying the first principles of God's oracles cannot grow to become the best in God's vineyard. No parent is happy seeing a two year old permanently fixed on milk. His growth will be stunted and eventually terminated. Some people have spent years in church, yet still need to be coerced and visited before they would come to church or attend to their duties. They still need to be pampered and sung lullabies before being encouraged to forget offences.

We cannot climb to the higher ground with energy solely from milk doctrines. We cannot be true labourers for Christ with our potential locked in milk. Without strong meat, there is no strong man. Drinking milk may present a posh picture with modern ambience for people, but when the harsh reality of faith hits and the storms arrive they will crash and crumble. Milk users are amateurs in faith: unskillful in handling the word of righteousness. It is not because they want to be amateurs, but because they are ignorant.

There are ministers on the podia today that are only known for using the milk of various attractions and motivations to feed their congregations. They use the milk of concerts, comedies and state of the art facilities to boost their numerical strength and the ignorant world tags them as successful. However, the Bible says that they use milk because they have no skills and no exposure to the word of righteousness. In this case, both the feeder and the fed are of the same stature and status before the Lord. It is a case of a toddler parenting a baby.

Strong Meat

Strong meat is the real deal. Higher ground is the transition from the milk diet to the strong meat buffet. It is for full age saints who are progressing in an upward direction to the place beyond the valleys. Strong meat does not belong to babes because it will choke them and alter their digestive systems spiritually. A friend invited to preach told me that his host begged him not to preach on or mention some themes in the Scriptures that dealt with sufferings and trials of faith. He was afraid the congregation would neither understand nor appreciate such teachings.

Some pastors are always afraid to bring fiery ministers to their congregations because they believe that the baby flock they have gathered for years will scatter. The wholesome words of Christ do not belong to baby churches and it is a threatening trend in twenty first century Christianity, as more babies are churned out to handle adult matters and responsibilities in the church. One crucial attribute of those feeding on strong meat is their ability to discern and differentiate between what is good and what is evil. It is not every evil that presents itself in a black appearance; some evil thoughts, ambitions, books, friends, goals, relationships and methods are wrapped in attractive containers. They cannot be recognized via mere observation or physical analysis but only through discernment. What a man feeds on affects how well his spiritual senses develop. A clear sense of direction on the path of life may not always come in the obvious colours of green means Go or red means Stop.

Distinguishing between an evil intentioned partner and an honest one may not come easily through simple observations of how long someone prays in unknown tongues, the whiteness of a pastor's collar, and the height of a Bishop 's cap or the absence of jewelries. The exercising of senses to discern and see what is not shown and hear what is not said may be the only sure test. Many people have been wrecked on their way up because they could not discern who to trust or who to abstain from. Abner could have become a topmost General in the Israeli Army under David but he could not discern a friendly hug from a deadly one.

Now when Abner returned to Hebron, Joab took him aside into an inner chamber, as if to speak with him privately. And there, to avenge the blood of his brother Asahel, Joab stabbed him in the stomach... (2 Samuel 3:27 NIV)

He had just left the palace safely and was called back by Joab who had a deadly intention. But how could Abner have suspected without the sense to discern? How would he know that despite securing favour with the king, there was someone nursing evil against him in the same kingdom, unknown even to the king? How would he know that staying where he was would be better than returning to where he had peacefully been previously? How would he know that Joab's quiet discussion was a cover for a deafening evil? You cannot go far in this dangerous cosmos without having discerning senses, which are developed from feeding on strong meat. You are what you eat! David mourned Abner in a profound dirge: "...should Abner have died as the lawless die? Your hands were not bound, your feet were not fettered. You fell as one falls before the wicked." And all the people wept over him again" (2 Samuel 3:34 NIV).

Abner's hands were not bound, his feet were not fettered, but his senses were not exercised to discern: he consequently fell before the wicked. There are wicked men who have mastered the art of felling people on their way up and to avoid them, you must discern them. It is not every quiet conversation that is peaceful.

Forgetting The Past

Brethren, I do not count myself to have apprehended; but one thing I do, forgetting those things that are behind and reaching forward to those things, which are ahead, I press toward the goal for the prize of the upward call of God in Christ Jesus. (Philippians 3:13-14 NKJV)

I Do Not Count Myself

Many people are not entering into higher ground in life as ordained for them by God because of how they regard themselves. With just a little achievement, they count themselves as chiefs of achievers, models, celebrities, yet all the while, they are in mediocrity. A little taste of progress blows some people off from the path of growth and they surrender their pursuit for growth. When some people become the first to bag a college degree in their families, they begin to walk around boastfully, full of pride. It is dangerous to overrate yourself; it keeps you from ascertaining what you actually weigh in life. The container is not a yardstick to determine the weight of the content.

The moment some ministers open their first parish or church, they become "papa" to their fathers and unreachable to their mates. There is a lot of packaging going on in the church and society these days, which drag men back from the true higher ground. They live in castles built in the air, expecting to earn reputations of height. What good is a height that lacks weight? If you must matter, you must have weight before occupying space. How easily do we count ourselves among the great, once we achieve a little above the common around us. It is often said that a young farmer who never visited the farm of his mate's father would assume his father's farmland is the biggest. It is amazing how some people rate themselves among the top, using the model of quantity and not quality.

When you place too much value on little achievements, you stop midway to higher ground. What have you apprehended that you now want to start your own parish? What have you apprehended in destiny that you now hire your mates to comb your hair? What have you apprehended that your mother's age mates must kneel down before they can speak with you? What have you apprehended that your title is bigger than your training in the things of God? What have you apprehended that no one can check your excesses or give you directives? You're now starting your own business simply because you have little savings without any competent experience. You brand your vehicle with a customized name just because you have some thousands from innocent people's tithes and offerings? That is why many young starters in the twenty-first century don't last. It is little wonder that many people who you expect so much from are delivering so little in God's economy. It is one of the reasons why people with high social ratings are caught in the same atrocities ensnaring people of lower reputations because they step into shoes of charisma without the sole of character.

To get into the higher ground, you cannot rest on your oars; you should never rest until your good is better and your better becomes best. I am not suggesting that you should not appreciate the landmarks in your life, but why would you go all out to celebrate killing a bird with a machine gun after a decade of hunting? Why would a man recruited into the vineyard of grace as a Sunday school teacher throw an extensive party before taking even the first class or winning one soul to Jesus?

This One Thing I Do

Focus is basic to a safe journey. All your activities in life must converge at a single purpose. It doesn't mean Paul was engaged in literally one single activity in his life, but everything he was doing centered on a push for the higher ground. Whatever had no bearing on his calling never caught his fancy, you could trace purpose in all his many parts. What unifies your diversity? How do the things you engage in, the job you're doing, the places you go and the relationships you keep, merge into one thing that defines your life? What is your focus before engaging in an endeavour?

The higher ground is reserved for those who have a united front in their pursuit for purpose. They are well targeted and focused. The pyramid of greatness may be founded on a wide base, but it must be pointed to a narrow end. What narrow future and eternity do your broad involvements point at? Anything that has no connection to the purpose of God for your life does not deserve your attention.

Paul pointed out a great ingredient of higher ground achievers in the kingdom: doing! He had cogent and tangible things he was doing. Higher ground is for doers not talkers. Many people die at the lower and undergrounds because they do nothing, but say much. What are you really doing? Paul had real evidence, things he could define and point to as what he was doing. Many people's achievements and efforts are in the realm of their thoughts and imaginations. They would not get down to working and making something meaningful happen through committed and articulated practice. The distinguishing feature of the first church leaders was not their titles or numbers, but their acts.

What are you doing to take your marriage up into the higher ground of bliss and love, instead of talking ill of your spouse or wishing them dead? What are you doing to promote godliness in your society apart from criticizing the leaders and ridiculing the followers? What are you doing to enforce kingdom principles at your workplace other than mourning the dilapidation of the moral infrastructure?

What are you doing to bring back our girls from cheap labour and sexual exploitation apart from watching their molestation on social media? What are you doing to save our boys from drug abuse and cultism other than sharing the videos of their atrocities? If a dictionary defines what you do, what would be the practical aspect of that definition? We can only climb the ladder of doing to higher ground.

Forgetting Those Things

It is often said that the greatest enemy of 'better' is 'good'. Where you have been is a bend on the road not an end of the road: good or bad. When we are occupied by 'those' things, things of today, we are empty of future things. The rich fool in Luke 12, died in his prime because he was engrossed in what had happened to his ground in terms of increase, and he refused to embrace what should happen in terms of impact in the future. He chose to expand his store instead of increasing his channels to reach more hungry souls. He didn't die because of a pressing present hunger; he died because of his past plenty.

For some, the negative past includes abuse and regrets. Joab brought a curse upon his children and family because he refused to let go of the war waged by Abner against David in the days of Saul. He murdered Abner in cold blood with a 'friendly' knife and David cursed him for that (See 2 Samuel chapter 3 NKJV).

Lot's wife became common street salt, not because she missed her way to the future but because she refused to let go of the past in Sodom. She looked back and became lifeless, static and common. Many marriages are not entering into the higher ground because the spouses are unforgiving: they still recall the offenses of the past and tenaciously hold on to where they came from. One of the clues to marital unity was given in Genesis chapter two verse twenty four: "That is why a man leaves his father and mother..." The father and mother represent where he came from, and he must leave them if he intends to unite with a new life.

The greatest issue that God had with the Israelites was their refusal to forget Egypt. Even though they were led out, they refused to let Egypt out from their mannerisms and orientations. The generation that came out of underground Egypt could not enter the higher ground of the Promised Land, with the exception of Caleb and Joshua, simply because they would not forget those things that were left behind in Egypt.

There are believers who have not entered into their full inheritance in Christ Jesus because they don't want to forget the past. Many Christians are backsliding because they refuse to forget about their past relationships and partners in crime. They still retain that old friend's number who ruined their sexual lives and financial fortunes in the game of pleasure. Some have not forgotten those worldly fashions, carnal elements in business, fraudulent contacts and contracts. What do you need to delete from your intellectual and spiritual memory cards? What do you need to format from your storage capacity? What offenses do you need to forget in order to follow peace? You cannot recollect those things of the past and understand the things of the future. You cannot be filled with the memory of what is temporal and expect to live in the eternal. What laurels do you need to forget and archive in your life's museum? The strength to achieve what is before you is to put the past behind you.

Reaching Forth Unto Those Things

Some things will not come to you in your village or on your bed of comfort. Higher ground cannot be relocated to your standard: you must reach forward for it. There are some higher things that you must reach for before you die. There are those things in ministry you must reach before breathing your last. There are things God planned for your marriage accomplish before death parts you and your spouse. You cannot experience the taste of higher ground until you reach some standards of living and raise the bar of your orientation.

There are spiritual heights and eternal weight you must gain before entering the higher ground. You cannot be living below the scriptural standard for your life and expect a lift into the supernatural. You cannot be operating your ministry below certain standards of integrity and expect the blessings that can be propagated into eternity. There are levels of studying you must reach before you can have a firm grip on the Word of Life, with the consequent effect of understanding the will of God.

Some people quit training in certain areas of their lives and never reached the certification stage, and as a result, they dropped out of relevance. Some cut off their journey to excellence in their profession and rather settled for an average service and substandard products. Some even saw best practices as too high, beyond their reach and rather settled for the common life. Higher ground requires some stretching and reaching out before breasting the tape.

Zacchaeus was of little stature according to the Scripture, but his intent was to see Jesus and to know who he was. Initially, he could not do it, because his height was below the strength of the crowd. He had every reason to complain about his height, since he was not the one who determined how tall he was. He could not by worry add even a cubit to his height. He could go back home and discuss with his family about the laudable idea of seeing Jesus in person, and throw a pity party, serving the wine of his natural disability. One would think that due to this kind of desire, God would instantly increase his height and increase his little stature to a mega stature. However, he reached out to his running capacity. He was short, but he was fast. God endows us with an advantage to balance any seeming disadvantage we may appear to have.

An African adage says that when God makes a man bald on the head, he compensates him with a beard on his face. He gained speed to run where others were walking and got ahead of them. Then, he reached out to climb a sycamore tree. He first tapped into his inner strength and then reached out to the outer support!

What race do you need to run now in your quest to reach the higher ground since you have a disadvantaged financial background or genetic makeup? Where in life do you need to double your pace ahead of others so that you can break even? What tree do you need to climb in order to have a clearer view of Jesus? What do you need to climb so your perspectives can be better? (Luke 19:3-40 NIV) In reaching forth, we must keep the right perspective for the things which are before; things ahead. You cannot put your gear on reverse and expect to move forward. There are those things in life that are positioned behind and there are those things that are in front. What you're reaching out for determines whether your life is going higher or lower. Progressive pursuits change our altitude. Chasing after what has passed or what is passing can never take you upward. Your search determines your reach: you cannot keep the expired in view and find the required. Anything worldly is behind, but the eternal is before and ahead. What is the eternal positioning of your pursuit and goals? Can your dreams be rewarded in eternity? What is the eternal value of your ambition?

Pressing Towards The Mark

The right mark is surrounded by forces of discouragement and compromise; no one walks into the higher ground leisurely. There is a pressing required against the wall of opposition in order to get to the new height you're trying to gain. Can you mount enough pressure on what is trying to delist you from the scroll of relevance? You need to press against the dark forces, towards the mark. Some people know how to mount pressure on their spouses towards relocation, fashion or ceremonies but not towards the mark. What mark is "the mark" in your life where you must continue to press towards?

What releases the prize is your getting to the mark, scoring the goal and hitting the target. You don't just fall onto the mark; you must press in to get there. Press in prayers, in studying, in meditation, enrolling for new courses, visiting places that contribute to your exposure, reading the right books and asking the right questions. Can you bear the pressure that comes with seeking the higher ground? How long can you survive the weight of pressing demands before caving in?

The prize is the consequence of applying the right pressure; it is a response to a high calling. Which calling are you responding to in life? Samuel's journey to the higher ground in his ministry didn't take off until he began to respond to God's calling and stopped running to Eli in error. You cannot keep answering to lower callings and end up in higher ground. Nobody will do the pressing for you. You cannot go far by relying on another person's pressing to bring down your own wall. You cannot solely depend on other people's prayers to open the doors of your destiny for you. In order to reach higher ground, you must burn like fire, pour like rain, gush like mighty waters, roar like thunder, scorch like the sun, strike like lightning and blow like the wind!

CHAPTER FOUR

The Transfiguration

After six days Jesus took with him Peter, James and John the brother of James, and led them up a high mountain by themselves. (Matthew 17:1 NIV)

After Six Days

How long have you spent in the process before gunning for the new realm? Humans are always attracted to the promise but reluctant about the process. There are things that only happen after some days of training and labouring. If your days are not fulfilled you cannot bring forth a term baby. There are so many arranged and packaged premature deliveries in destinies today because they enter into the delivery room before the expected day of delivery. The seventh day of rest came for God after the six days of labour and commitment to the new order. Your lifting is tied to a time appointed by the Father and there is nothing you can do to make a baby come to full term in three months. There are doors that God will not open until after "six days." This also applies to opportunities, privileges, accesses and exposures. Waiting time is not a wasting season; rather, it's more of preparation for the coming demands. God is not in a hurry to lift any man until he has fulfilled his days. You don't sow a seed and start opening it up daily, with the hope of having it come up instantly. Those who apply to God for instant miracles will never be selected in God's recruitment processes into the Higher Ground. Getting things early is not primary to God, but getting you ready is.

Are you on the first, second, third, fourth, fifth or sixth day? God will not delay you longer than planned except you have skipped classes during the days of your preparation. The birth of John was miraculous, the prophecy over his life was heavy, signs around his birth were divine and he had the message locked in his heart, but he was banished into the deserts until the days of his showing unto Israel (Luke1:80). Things are only beautiful in God's time. Don't seek for things to happen before your time.

Taken by Jesus

Who is taking you up? Many people pride themselves in being self-made while others ascribe their success to their parents or relatives. In actual fact, God will use people to assist your rising to the peak of God purpose for your life, but the brain behind true lifting is Jesus. You cannot get to the higher ground without being taken there by Jesus because it is in him, by him and for him that all things consist; and God has made Jesus the Head for the church. All heights and influence dwell in him. Stop struggling to make things happen by yourself without involving Jesus, he is the only person that can take you up and keep you there. Stop running after people to take you up into the higher ground.

Many people have missed their turns for lifting because they have been taken away by others or by their own schemes and schedules. Don't jump the gun, put your hands in his hands and allow to walk you up the mountains into the height of glory. So many ministers have been taken in by money or business and those things hinder them from becoming who God wanted them to be. There are ministers who have been taken away from Jesus' hands and from where they would have been taken up to a higher ground, by their selfish ambitions, friends or greed.

Who is currently taking you around? Who is posting you to where you're working? Who is determining your direction in life? Who has seized the freedom bequeathed through the saving grace of Christ from you? Don't worry if the speed is slow with Jesus, don't be destabilized if it reduces your freedom to fraternize with others; going with Jesus is a sure way up.

If Jesus is the one taking you, he will bring with you, men of like passion and like minds. Don't select who should go up with you; it may be a snare used by the enemy to scuttle your journey, let Jesus do the selection. Many people in the name of networking have found themselves underground in destiny. Don't lobby to win people's cooperative hands in business, ministry or marriage. It was not all the disciples that Jesus took with him to the mount of transfiguration, but only three. The way up does not have space for everybody and only Jesus knows who best fits into the higher ground where you're headed.

Bringing Them Up

It is not enough to be under control, we must also be properly brought up. Many people fail to rise to higher ground because they don't like to be properly brought up. It is alarming to see many young people climbing the high mountains in ministry, business and power without proper upbringing. The decadence on the podia today and the immorality among the board members in multinational corporations can be traced to wrong upbringing. It accounts for why many promising young men are falling professionally from grace to grass. Who are you accountable to on the way up? Who scolds you and holds you en route to greatness?

There are character build-ups and contributions that must take place on the way up and it cannot happen after getting there. It is when some people get married that they begin to learn how to cook. Many young undergraduates do not know how to live decently while under the immediate watch of their parents and therefore, live loosely at the first taste of freedom.

Ultimately, we must allow our minds and character to be brought up to the level that Christ expects of us. We must be developed in the spirit and mind to the capacity fitting for the upward life. You cannot afford to be an intellectual dwarf at the height of success. The real higher ground requires the company of Jesus. You cannot locate the higher ground without him bringing you there.

Apart

Coming into the higher ground carries the consequence of separation, a need to be set apart. One battle that many people have found perpetually impossible is separation. They want to keep the old company and still get a new comfort, keep the old habit and find a new life, retain the old wrong friends and build a brand new force. They love to keep the old wineskin but thirst for a new wine. Being set apart is not a demonstration of superiority but a commitment to keeping and sustaining the new life.

For some people, they need a severing deliverance in order to be set apart from their phones. They cannot do without pressing the phone even in the church or before a dignitary. This habit has crashed many homes and ruined many students' academic pursuits. Some people need to be set apart from television and movies. They can wake and bake before the screen from dawn to dusk, doing nothing but watching and eating.

There are those who need to be separated from food and drinks: they can never joke with their stomach infrastructure; their belly is their god. There are ladies who need to be set apart from cravings for jewelry and fashion. They only derive self-worth from what they put on the body. They can spend hours dressing without getting bored but they cannot take a few minutes before the mirror of God's word and not fall asleep. Some people cannot set themselves apart from attending social functions on a weekend in order to attend a retreat with brethren and pray.

What have you found extremely impossible to live without? It may be your strongest hindrance to a new height in glory. There are men who would have built multimillion-dollar businesses if not for their union with automobiles and ladies. They splurge everything they earn on cars and ladies even at the detriment of their families and dreams. Being with Jesus on the high mountain meant this to the disciples: separation.

No one serving as a soldier gets entangled in civilian affairs, but rather tries to please his commanding officer. (2 Timothy 2:4 NIV)

Getting to the higher ground is like a war. Have you come to terms with that reality in your quest for greatness? Becoming who God intends you to be is not a party experience for merry-makers but a war fought strategically and spiritually, especially in the battlefield of the mind. If your approach to life is not as serious as being on a war front, you're already defeated.

You have to fight your flesh and resist it to the end, fight the devil fiercely with the whole armour of God, fight the world system with the witness of righteousness and fight discouragement from those who have no idea about God's counsel for your life. To fight successfully, the first enemy to conquer is the entanglement called "affairs of this life." It has crippled many destinies from rising up; it has sent some people into jail and brought some people's finances down on its belly. Just to measure up socially, some people enter into debt and spend more than they earn in order to impress people and reflect with glitters in the social mirror. People throw wedding parties with borrowed money and plunge their marriage into the flood of regrets while servicing debts.

How many ministers have ruined their integrity with the building affairs since the social yardstick for success are the physical buildings you have on the ground?! People spend the money they don't have on things they don't need to impress people they don't know. What is entangling your fight to greatness? Some have become ruined in transit camps in northern Africa as slaves and many are dead because they wanted to cross into Europe in false hopes of greener pasture. They want to level up socially as being foreign-based and push their profile up in society. What does it cost you to measure up with the affairs of this life? There are women who fight their husbands for social uniforms even at the risk of ruining the future of their children. It is sad to know how much of the church income goes into the "affairs of this life" by general overseers in securing titles from the college of bishops and other unscriptural associations.

So many sharp battle-axes are now blunt through unholy relationships with politicians and rich fools. The truth has been diluted by the waters of compromise in the mouth of threshing instruments. We see no more of our cutting edge signs of revival flaming and the sparkling beauty of purity known within the faith of Christ. Churches now consult marketers and social media promoters to enhance the image and identity of their set men and secure lucrative patronage from society and the corridors of power. The affairs of this life have choked the life of Christ from many ministries and put out their flames. An entangled man cannot please him who has chosen him to be a soldier. How can you be brought up into the higher ground without pleasing the Lord who will lead you there? How can you expect to be promoted by your Commander when you always grieve his heart? Choosing God over your life as a Christian is to abandon the carnal civilian life of pleasure and embrace the smart, structured spiritual life in the army of the Lord. You have been chosen to be a soldier: a fighter, a warrior, a defender of faith, employing a no-nonsense lifestyle in extending and enforcing the kingdom of righteousness. A life that only carries the needed weapons and artilleries and nothing more; a simple life that waits on command and obeys orders from above!

...let us throw off everything that hinders and the sin that so easily entangles. And let us run with perseverance the race marked out for us, fixing our eyes on Jesus... (Hebrews 12:1-2 NIV)

There are weights you cannot take to new heights. The way to higher ground is narrow and cannot accommodate some worldly and ungodly weights. Those weights are stumbling blocks on the way up and the best place to lay them is aside: away from the way. They could be animate weights or inanimate burdens. Included on the list are easy sins that do not require rehearsal before practicing them. Sins that are native to your nature and orientations have been easily practiced by you for so long, they don't even feel or seem like sins to you anymore.

Do you have the courage and desire to lay aside such sins that have helped you make more money in business over the years and given you an inflated reputation among the brethren? It is upon getting rid of the weight and sins that we gain momentum to run with patience (character) the race that is set before us. The message here is that you must learn to travel light if you want to go far. Some things are not needed on your journey up: some friends, acquisitions, materials, titles and yokes are just distractions from the main point.

Having been free, adjust your lens that you don't copy the wrong examples in an effort towards getting to the place of greatness and becoming who God wants you to be. Many young people set out with sincere intentions to run the race of business and ministry with character but were looking to a wrong leader. They eventually went off on a tangent outside their true purpose. Jesus will never fade away in the darkness or disappear in the storm; he is always present and bold with the right example to follow no matter the sharp bends or curves.

Dig Your Well

Isaac reopened the wells that had been dug in the time of his father Abraham, which the Philistines had stopped up after Abraham died... (Genesis 26:18 NIV)

A lot of people jumped to easy conclusions on the great harvest reaped by Isaac during the famine of his days. Every profit over our labour is a reflection of divine permission, since the race is not granted to the swift nor bread to the wise. However, a more important reality that unlocked the harvest for Isaac was the principle he adopted which was to irrigate his own farmland.

While others were waiting for the rain to fall naturally from heaven, Isaac was wise to dig water out from the ground. He reopened the wells; repeating what worked for his father, walking in the footsteps of the patriarch of faith. One great lesson from Isaac to the modern youths who aspire to get into the higher ground is to walk in the godly footsteps of the fathers. Many young people are missing the right turns to greatness because they abandon the truthful old principles for the fanciful lies of modernization. Repeating the successful lifestyle of his father was what sustained Isaac when waters were no longer pouring through rain. The wells were blocked by envious Philistines who felt Isaac was too young for the kind of success he was handling at his tender age. They couldn't handle how God blessed him, how he waxed great, went forward and grew until he became very great. As natural conditions threatened the blessings over his life, he began to dig wells again without laying back and complaining about the natural disaster.

It is not in every season that you have to clear clouds along the way to success, but you must understand what works and what does not. What well do you need to dig again? There are wells of knowledge that need to be dug, wells of wisdom and studies. Don't sit back wailing when the rain of free opportunities no longer falls. There is water beneath the surface that famine cannot stop. You just need to unearth the water by removing the hard soil until you hit the fountain beneath. There is a pool of sustenance for crossing the bars of limitations from surviving to thriving that only hard diggers can reach.

Isaac repeatedly dug and the enemies continued to block the wells because they knew it was the key to greatness. Some people have the capacity to spoil but no strength to preserve. They only give envious attention to those labouring to improve their own impact on earth. Once you go down like them, they will keep your friendship, but the moment you begin to put in extra effort to overcome limitations for yourself, they start to block your chances for testimonies. Isaac overcame by digging again, and again until he reached Rehoboth; the capacity to dig eventually overwhelmed the strength to block.

Can you continue without relenting until the enemy is brought under control? What weakens the enemy is your consistency in getting things right in life. Who gives up first: you or the enemy? A man going higher keeps at repeating the digging no matter the cost, until he breaks even.

The make-believe packaging of the gospel has succeeded at being silent on the well digging efforts of Isaac in bringing in a bumper harvest during famine. It is instead focused on the fact that the harvest was mysteriously supernatural. God sustains the earth by principles and intervenes occasionally by miracles. Getting to the higher ground is not a miraculous escape from the ordinary to extraordinary; it is a stepwise commitment to go beyond the surface in pursuing the life of impact. Where are you diggers? It is time to start digging your own wells because every generation would have its own famine and so, they must dig their own well.

Digging means reaching for depth; depth is the only force that sustains height. You cannot be scratching the surface in life and survive the famine of your generation.

You cannot be a surface person and suddenly wax great. Many ministries are running out of steam today because they only depend on narratives in pamphlets to train members and workers in these times of spiritual famine. There is a grueling scarcity in our days and it is clear that only a digging ministry will outlast these perilous times. Many marriages are famished because the spouses are surface providers; they only bond in the flesh and not in the bones. They only share the same bed, but not the bread of life. They invest on the outward and decay inward, draining the family of joyful moisture.

CHAPTER FIVE

Hannah's Journey

To The Higher Ground

Because the Lord had closed Hannah's womb, her rival kept provoking her in order to irritate her. This went on year after year. Whenever Hannah went up to the house of the Lord, her rival provoked her till she wept and would not eat. (1 Samuel 1:6-7, NIV)

Your life cannot be studied in the college of impact unless you have passed through the grades of God's dealings. Those who escape training have consequently avoided reigning. It is okay to think of fibroids preventing Hannah from conceiving or other medical issues in her or her husband. However, how can we embrace the reality exposed by the Scripture that it was the Lord who closed Hannah's womb? When God intends to open you to certain lessons in life, He can close some doors. No matter your efforts at opening them, they remain shut because He alone holds the key of David; He opens and no man can shut, He shuts and no man can open (see Revelation 3: 7 NIV). Many times we run to God when our world is shaking only to find out on getting to him that He is the One doing the shaking. What can you do when it is God who is preventing you from getting pregnant, from getting a visa, from getting a job from getting a spouse? God's delay is not God's denial; He chooses when we have what, according to His eternal counsel.

Those moments when God is delaying responses to your prayers usually feel like underground moments in life and except you come out strong by aligning with His plans; you may delay your exit to the next level. It cost God nothing to bless Abraham with children in accordance to His promise, but God had a specific time in mind and faith was in the curriculum to teach father Abraham. In Abraham's attempt to open the schildbearing door, he ended up in a mess that served as a thorn in the flesh of His promise. There is a shape you must take in the spirit through the trials before God can trust you with the higher ground.

Provocation

Next in the syllabus was provocation for Hannah through Penninah her rival. The underground experience is a stage of provocation and irritation. Everything around your life will stir uneasiness within you during underground days. Some people wouldn't have had the privilege of insulting and ridiculing you if not for God's purposeful delay in answering some prayers. Sometimes, it feels like those who don't need much have surplus while those in dire need are languishing in lack. Some people have the habit of blaming others for disadvantages that were not caused by the victims. Some abuse you for the shape of your head as if you made it so.

There are limitations in our lives that had nothing to do with our shortcomings or errors, but which those in competition with us, use against us. The test is aimed at determining what our reactions would look like. There are some prayers you wouldn't have prayed if not for the provocations in your life. Some people wouldn't have created time to go on marathon fasts if not for certain provocations from people who felt they were better than them. There are courses we wouldn't have taken if not for the provocation at the workplace; some people wouldn't have worked harder if not for the provocation of bills.

You have to break through opposition in order to experience a breakthrough. There can be no Jesus Christ without the cross; Paul also had Alexander the coppersmith. Joseph had his eleven siblings to stir him into the fulfillment of his dreams. He was a daddy's boy in Jacob's household and enjoying it until he was thrown into prison and sold into slavery by his siblings.

Your reaction to your Peninnah in life is what determines the length of your stay in that class and the ground that you're currently operating from. Never react to your Peninnah with anger, but with prayer. Also never react to your Peninnah with bitterness but see her as someone positioned in your destiny path to make you a better person. Furthermore, never think you can change your Peninnah. You can only change your reaction or attitude but not a Peninnah. Trying to change your Peninnah will worsen the situation and will keep you under his or her control.

You need those provocations to push you back to God and draw you closer into His embrace. You need those people who look down on you with disdain so that you can look up to God for help. You need those provocations from people who have much and are expected to cater for those who don't but rather decide to oppress them, even in the church. Hannah's provocation test went on for many years and became a routine for the adversary to celebrate a festival with. How do you cope with people who are happy at your tears because of something that God personally blocked you from having? It is easy if it is only a one-off thing, but for Hannah, it was an annual routine. She was saddest during the marrying season. The weights of our pains are increased when we are surrounded by people who capitalize on our lacks for their laughs. Hannah was provoked until she was deprived of joy and her appetite. The reason why the adversary provokes you is to starve you of your soul and body meals.

How you react to provocation determines how you emerge from it. Running from such challenges with your head bowed down extends your distance to divine solutions. What are you doing about the provocations in your life? What have you deprived yourself of because someone doesn't like your face or refuses to understand your gracious enrolment in the divine college?

A story was told of a farmer's donkey which went astray until it fell into a pit where people in the neighbourhood dumped their refuse and wastes.

The donkey couldn't help itself out and no matter how loud it brayed, no one would help it out. Before long, people started dumping refuse into the pit and consequently on it. He reasoned as to what he could do. He had two options: either to be there while they gradually buried him underground or to shake the refuse off and step on it. He opted to shake it off. So, each time anyone came around to dump refuse in the pit, the donkey would shake it off and step on it.

Eventually, he noticed that the refuse was gradually taking him up as he stepped on it. It became his only way out: shaking it off and stepping on it. The donkey eventually came up and walked out triumphantly.

We must learn to shake off some provocations and step on them. The oxygen that expands the lungs of our adversaries is when we react with attention and self-pity. Hannah was going to the house of the Lord and yet she was giving more attention to the issues around her life. Is it not funny that some issues will not hinder us from performing certain duties for the Lord, yet they will block us from getting the most from our intimacy with Christ? Don't allow anyone to rob you of the fullness of joy that can only be fetched in His presence.

If you reason with an arrogant cynic, you'll get slapped in the face; confront bad behavior and get a kick in the shins. So don't waste your time on a scoffer; all you'll get for your pains is abuse. But if you correct those who care about life, that's different—they'll love you for it! Save your breath for the wise—they'll be wiser for it; tell good people what you know—they'll profit from it. Skilled living gets its start in the Fear-of-God, insight into life from knowing a Holy God. It's through me, Lady Wisdom, that your life deepens, and the years of your life ripen. Live wisely and wisdom will permeate your life; mock life and life will mock you. (Proverbs 9:7, 8, MSG)

Experts have described the birth of a pearl as miraculous. Unlike gemstones, which are cut and polished to bring out their luster, pearls are naturally born from oysters with a complete radiance and a soft, lustrous, inner glow. It begins as an irritant lodged in an oyster's soft inner body where it is impossible to expel. In reaction to this irritant, the oyster's body starts to secrete a smooth, hard crystalline substance around the irritant in self-defense. The substance secreted is referred to as "nacre" which is produced continually in layer upon layer. With time, the irritant is completely enclosed by the silky crystalline coatings, which ultimately turn out to become our lovely pearl.

Hannah's Positive Response

In her deep anguish, Hannah prayed to the Lord, weeping bitterly. And she made a vow, saying, "Lord Almighty, if you will only look on your servant's misery and remember me, and not forget your servant but give her a son, then I will give him to the Lord for all the days of his life, and no razor will ever be used on his head." (1 Samuel 1:10, 11, NIV)

PRAYERS

When we are in deep hardship, we must respond with a deep intercession to the Lord. Prayer is a critical response to provocation. A prayerful woman may have seasons of bitterness and anguish, but she will never take her matters to the social media for help but to the Lord in prayers. Her weeping may endure for a night; joy will surely come in the morning.

We must be wise in discerning who to talk to in crises in order not to complicate the problem. Many women seeking for fruits of the womb have been swindled by fake prophets who exploited them emotionally and financially. Some were converted to sex objects with threats against disclosure; others were even converted to become second wives to the prophet while many homes have consequently been broken. There are even women who were murdered by the same people they sought to cure their barrenness.

Men in financial barrenness have also been taken advantage of by fraudsters who took the little they had in promise of a great financial freedom. The urge towards seeking quick cures to challenges tend to push people around and about to ridiculous extents, eventually multiplying their own sorrows. Who are you talking to? Have you been so overwhelmed by your challenges that praying has become a boring burden on your agenda?

We often suffer many pains because we do not always commit everything to God in prayers.

VOW

It is critical to note that Hannah was not making a vow to the Lord with an attitude of adding to God's net worth. Some believers have the wrong attitude in the place of vows to God. They do it as if they are doing God a favour. Such arrogant vows are not acceptable to the Lord. Hannah saw herself as a servant and handmaid who had no leverage except mercy from her Master.

Her vow also shows that she is not selfish: not seeking a son for social brag or tag. If given, she offered back the son to the Giver. She would give the son permanently and properly to God. Some people make revocable vows with a window to escape from fulfilling it. There are others who give things to God but are not consecrated wholly to Him. She promised to keep him from being shaven as a Nazarite.

Vows are critical in our walk with God, to show our readiness to partner with His project and our commitment to His person more than His presents. Vows show that we are ready to release what we have received, which qualifies us for more releases. God doesn't bless dams that keep back but He increases rivers with outflow channels. Indicate a sign of commitment in your relationship with God by fulfilling those vows and it will amaze you what God can do.

HONOUR

When a dying Prophet Eli erroneously perceived that Hannah was drunk, one would think Hannah would be angry. Hannah still esteemed and reverenced Eli." Hannah was praying in her heart, and her lips were moving but her voice was not heard. Eli thought she was drunk and said to her, "How long are you going to stay drunk? Put away your wine." "Not so, my lord," Hannah replied, "I am a woman who is deeply troubled. I have not been drinking wine or beer; I was pouring out my soul to the Lord" (1 Samuel 1:13-15 NIV).

Many people have blocked their way to higher ground due to provocation from people who should know better but misunderstood them. Here, her 'mentor' became her 'tormentor' and she still maintained her cool. She had a deep trouble but she didn't allow that to uproot her tree of honour.

When some people are annoyed or provoked, they go to any length to insult and drag even the anointed of God in the mud of disregard; everybody around them during the anger season is seen as inconsequential. She took her time to state her deep trouble and clarified her sane state to the spiritually dim prophet. It is not about the person of Eli but the position he occupied among God's people as the anointed. It was at this point of honour that she received the prophetic word for her higher ground in childbearing. Peace and promise were invoked upon her by Eli. Honour is one of the keys to receiving from God. A similar scenario occurred in a dialogue between Jesus and the Syro-Phoenician woman in the gospel according to Mark:

"From there Jesus set out for the vicinity of Tyre. He entered a house there where he didn't think he would be found, but he couldn't escape notice. He was barely inside when a woman who had a disturbed daughter heard where he was. She came and knelt at his feet, begging for help. The woman was Greek, Syro-Phoenician by birth. She asked him to cure her daughter. He said, "Stand in line and take your turn. The children get fed first. If there's any left over, the dogs get it." She said, "Of course, Master. But don't dogs under the table get scraps dropped by the children?" (Mark 7:24-28, MSG)

Jesus called the woman a dog! The woman was not angry but instead honoured Jesus. Many level ground people honour with their mouth or lips and forget that honour is a thing of the heart. Some still fight those that have authority over them. Some complain about the words and attitude of their leaders. Some are rude, crude, and use foul languages against their leaders/ Pastors. Hannah's honour was true and genuine. It was from her heart; a wise man said; "you cannot attract what you attack."

HUMILITY

She said, "May your servant find favour in your eyes." Then she went her way and ate something, and her face was no longer downcast. (I Samuel 1:18 NIV)

Hannah's humility allowed her to accept the ministry of the prophet despite the wrong first impression. Some rude women would have reasoned within themselves that a prophet who couldn't discern a drunken woman from a sorrowful woman could not accurately invoke the blessing of God and see it come to pass. She could have despised him, if not for her humble spirit. She received the word with meekness of heart and it was profitable to her. Many people have missed their promotions in life because of the wrong impressions they incubated concerning the minister that God intended to use for their breakthrough. Perceiving that the pastor doesn't drive a particular type of car, dress in a particular way or speak in a pre-conceived way, they disdain his ministry and consequently shoot themselves in the feet.

FAITH

Hannah also took steps of faith by walking away like an expectant employee who has gotten a payment alert of her salary and headed out to the ATM for withdrawal. The pregnancy didn't jump into her immediately, but she received it in her spirit instantly. She had assurance of her hope and evidence of the things she could not yet see. The journey to higher ground is fueled by faith; we can only relate with God on our level of faith and thereby, move up by the same faith. God wants you to walk out of prayer sessions with deep convictions and assurance that what you've asked for according to His will shall be released. She became agile by faith and refused to be locked down again. She ate to build up strength for what God had promised to do.

You don't wait until it happens before starting to build stamina for the coming blessing. Don't wait until the monthly cycle is missed before eating for strength and knowledge to know how to handle what God is bringing your way. Eat, the journey to the higher ground is far and God is determined to take you there if you will eat His Word as the bread of life and will not faint.

Hannah put off the sad mood as if the miracle had already landed; you cannot be bitter and be better. True faith must influence your mood and emotions. Wear the best costume of a smile in confidence of what God would do in your life. Smile at the storm, wave at the wind, rejoice and again rejoice because the joy of the Lord is your strength. Don't give the devil such privilege to deplete your vault of joy.

GRATITUDE

Hannah's gratitude was not silent. She burst out in exuberance praise of God. Her evergreen song says it all as recorded in 1 Samuel 2:2 KJV, "There is none holy as the LORD: for there is none beside thee: neither is there any rock like our God." The social philosopher, Eric Hoffer, says, "The hardest arithmetic to master is that which enables us to count our blessings." When you operate from higher ground, your praise and thanksgiving is irrepressible. Your life is all about God and not yourself. You're dependable for God, you depend on God and you live a lifestyle of gratitude. Gladys Bertha Stern, the British author, also wrote, "Silent gratitude isn't much use to anyone."

Hannah moved from level ground to higher ground and remained there perpetually in grand style. She didn't display superiority through rascality or arrogance with the aim of getting even with her rival. She followed the process of the promise and consequently got transformed by the renewal of her mind. She displayed characteristics of those on higher ground:

1. SACRIFICE

She willingly offered her first son to God. This is similar to what Abraham did on Mount Moriah with Isaac and what God did by sacrificing His only begotten Son, Jesus Christ to come to this world of sin to redeem us.

Now when she had weaned him, she took him up with her, with three bulls, one ephah of flour, and a skin of wine, and brought him to the house of the Lord in Shiloh. And the child was young. Then they slaughtered a bull, and brought the child to Eli. And she said, "O my lord! As your soul lives, my lord, I am the woman who stood by you here, praying to the Lord. For this child I prayed, and the Lord has granted me my petition which I asked of Him. Therefore I also have lent him to the Lord; as long as he lives he shall be lent to the Lord." So they worshiped the Lord there. (1 Samuel 1: 24-28 NKJV)

This is an ultimate sacrifice. Hannah's focus was no longer on herself, but on God. This sacrifice proved her unconditional love for God. You can give without love but you cannot love without giving. When you're truly on the higher ground, your sacrifices to God increase and improve. Those who complain about tight schedules and demands as reasons for not making huge sacrifices for God are yet to experience the higher ground in their life's journey.

2. SONG OF PRAISE/WORSHIP

Hannah became a true worshipper. Her worship was no longer restricted to Shiloh. It became a habit. Hannah's song of praise showed her continuous heart of worship. Hannah prayed:

"The LORD has filled my heart with joy; how happy I am because of what he has done! I laugh at my enemies; how joyful I am because God has helped me! No one is holy like the LORD; there is none like him, no protector like our God. Stop your loud boasting; silence your proud words. For the LORD is a God who knows, and he judges all that people do. The bows of strong soldiers are broken, but the weak grow strong. The people who once were well fed now hire themselves out to get food, but the hungry are hungry no more. The childless wife has borne seven children, but the mother of many is left with none. The LORD kills and restores to life; he sends people to the world of the dead and brings them back again. He makes some people poor and others rich; he humbles some and makes others great. He lifts the poor from the dust and raises the needy from their misery. He makes them companions of princes and puts them in places of honour. The foundations of the earth belong to the LORD; on them he has built the world. "He protects the lives of his faithful people, but the wicked disappear in darkness; a man does not triumph by his own strength. The LORD's enemies will be destroyed; he will thunder against them from heaven. The LORD will judge the whole world; he will give power to his king, he will make his chosen king victorious." (1 Samuel 2:1-10, GNT)

In this song, Hannah adored and affirmed God as a Rock that is firm, strong, reliable and immovable. Worship improves your perspective about God; it opens your spirit to the reality and capacity of God in an amplified manner. Hannah's song can be compared to Mary's own rendition as recorded in Luke 1:46-55 GNT:

Mary said, "My heart praises the Lord; my soul is glad because of God my Savior, for he has remembered me, his lowly servant! From now on all people will call me happy, because of the great things the Mighty God has done for me. His name is holy; from one generation to another he shows mercy to those who honour him. He has stretched out his mighty arm and scattered the proud with all their plans. He has brought down mighty kings from their thrones, and lifted up the lowly. He has filled the hungry with good things, and sent the rich away with empty hands. He has kept the promise he made to our ancestors, and has come to the help of his servant Israel. He has remembered to show mercy to Abraham and to all his descendants forever!"

Higher ground makes your lips productive and causes your heart to rejoice. You turn out spontaneous melodies and flow in the lyrics of gratitude. You won't a push from anyone before you release albums containing fresh songs of gratitude to the Lord even if you're the only fan of your music.

Hannah kept thanking God. Her thanksgiving portrays the spirit of faith and faith moves the hand of God. No wonder she was blessed with five other children.

The LORD did bless Hannah, and she had three more sons and two daughters. The boy Samuel grew up in the service of the LORD. (1 Samuel 2:21, GNT)

Hannah knew that until you thank God, your miracle is not complete. This is in line with the Samaritan leper who was healed with the other nine lepers by Jesus. Only the Samaritan came back to thank God. He was the one Jesus pronounced whole. The other nine were healed but not completely whole.

Jesus asked, "Were not all ten cleansed? Where are the other nine? Has no one returned to give praise to God except this foreigner?" Then he said to him, "Rise and go; your faith has made you well." (Luke 17:17-19, NIV)

Hannah instituted memorials. She went to Shiloh yearly. She never left the temple. She gave generously to Samuel. The birth of Samuel was a significant thing God had done in her life and she took care of the gift of God.

But Samuel was ministering before the Lord—a boy wearing a linen ephod. Each year his mother made him a little robe and took it to him when she went up with her husband to offer the annual sacrifice. (1 Samuel 2:18 - 19, NIV)

Hannah never lived a life of complaints again. She quit complaining totally. Her focus was on God. She realized that complaining complicates matters. Complaining makes one stink and miserable like the Psalmist puts it:

I remembered you, God, and I groaned; I meditated, and my spirit grew faint." (Psalm 77:3, NIV)

Olayinka Dada, M.D.

Worry never removes the challenges of tomorrow but it saps today of its strength. You cannot be worried and be worthy of the next level. When gratitude is your attitude, you come into beatitude among the multitude with an altitude.

Final Notes

What type of ground are you currently on? Never accept any ground short of higher ground. Do not let your past hold you back from climbing higher. The past may consist of failure, hurt, disappointment, mistakes, errors, sins etc. You may need to break loose from your past and move to the future with hope in God. Remember the past is in the tomb, while tomorrow is in the womb. Also, ignore your critics who are trying to tie you into one spot. Be focused on the height you're designed to reach.

Learn to count your blessings; it is one of the secrets for climbing and sustaining the higher ground. Focus on what God has done. If you think deeply you will be grateful. God is in charge of your seasons. If not for God, you would have been six feet under.

The secret is to live a life of thankfulness. Let gratitude become your lifestyle. The password and key to remain in the presence of God is thanksgiving.

Enter with the password: "Thank you!" Make yourselves at home, talking praise. Thank him. Worship him. (Psalm 100:4, MSG)

Thanksgiving helps us build and solidify our relationship with God. It connotes total dependence on God. David gave thanks at all times. Paul also lived a life of gratitude. Jesus also gave thanks always. No wonder, Paul admonished us to, "give thanks in all circumstances; for this is God's will for you in Christ Jesus." (1 Thessalonians 5:18, NIV)

EVERYTHING IS EVERYTHING!

The way up is down. Don't just be quick to embrace the promise of the higher ground and denounce the process. You cannot be the product if you avoid the process. Statistics may not favour your current or past realities, but God doesn't consult facts before determining the future. It is not where we come from that determines where we are going to, rather it is what we have come through.

If you cannot manage the distress of humble beginnings, you cannot be trusted with heights. God focuses first on who we are before he ushers us into where we should be. Separate yourself, watch your association. Associations are like an elevator, they either take you down or take you higher. You must know when to operate in the gift of goodbye with some of your associates.

You must realize that the pyramid of growth is smaller as you grow up in capacity. The chains on Peter when Herod held him did not drop until he rose up. Some chains of wrong friendships naturally drop off when you raise the bar of your mindset to be Christ-like. You cannot combine pleasing men and satisfying God.

Blessed is the one who does not walk in step with the wicked or stand in the way that sinners take or sit in the company of mockers. (Psalm 1:1, NIV)

Stay separate from the wicked, sinners and mockers. Face the reality that you cannot change people. Do not get entangled with people and with their ungodly ways of life.

SUSTAINING THE HIGHER GROUND

Acquiring the higher ground is one thing, sustaining the momentum to get there and stay there is another ball game entirely. Standards are easier to achieve than to maintain. Many athletes take off well but drop behind during the race because they lack the energy to keep the same pace over time. For higher ground to not become past tense in the dictionary of your reality, you cannot afford to lower your guard or compromise the due process. You need to do whatever it takes in the context of God's will to remain perpetually on higher ground.

Bon voyage!

Printed in the United States
By Bookmasters